Landmark
BOOKS

D1030979

PETER STUYVESANT
OF OLD NEW YORK

PETER STUYVESANT

of Old New York

by **ANNA & RUSSEL CROUSE**

illustrated by Jo Spier

Landmark
BOOKS

RANDOM HOUSE • NEW YORK

CONTENTS

PETER STUYVESANT
OF OLD NEW YORK

1

DISCOVERY

WHEN our story begins, more than three hundred years ago, the world was much smaller than it is now—that is, what we call the civilized world. Many lands had not been discovered yet. Our own America hadn't been known long, and little was known about it.

One of the richest and most important nations of that day was the Netherlands. It was as small on the map as it is now, but it was great be-

Dutch ships poked their noses into every port

cause its ships sailed the seven seas and poked their square noses into every port, no matter what size, buying and selling. Their task was to find new ports, for ports meant new riches for which to trade. Trade meant wealth and power.

It was not strange, then, that every Dutch boy dreamed of the day when he would be a ship's captain. Perhaps he would be his country's hero, who, with his square-rigged sailing vessel, would find a new and easy sea lane to the East. From the Indies in the East ships returned with gold and ivory and jewels and spices.

The son of Dominie Balthazar Stuyvesant was no exception. On this September day in 1609 in the little town of Scherpenzeel, it is safe to say young Peter sailed his toy boat on one of the many canals that crisscrossed his native land. Perhaps it was just a wooden shoe with a handkerchief sail; for his father, being a minister, was poor.

Three thousand miles away, on that same September day, another boat—this one a real sailing vessel—pushed into a harbor in the New World. Its captain, standing on the quarter-deck, saw an island of majestic beauty lying between two great rivers—fourteen thousand acres of rock, lakes, and rolling land. Tall sturdy oaks and sycamores, pines and hemlocks rose above a junglelike growth of wild roses and blackberries, grapes and flowering shrubs.

Here was no ordinary island. The captain of the ship sensed this at once.

"It is as beautiful as the foot of man ever trod upon," he wrote that night in the ship's log.

It was to be much more than that. Man would replace nature's beauty with a beauty of his own designing—towering buildings to replace tower-

ing trees and a jungle of twisting traffic to sup-
plant intertwined vines and bushes.

For the ship's captain was Henry Hudson. And
the island he had found in his search for the Indies was Manhattan. On it was to rise the city
of New York, richer even than the Indies.

Peter Stuyvesant must have heard stories of this
new land, for the ship that found it, even though
not looking for it, was a Dutch ship called
the *Half Moon*. Young Peter was to know this
island well in later years and it was to know
him. But many things were to happen first,
both to the island and to Peter.

The *Half Moon* was a Dutch boat, but Henry
Hudson, its captain, was an Englishman.

He was one of the great sailors of his time, a
fearless man who was so fine a navigator that his
sailors said of him:

"He has a compass in his head."

The true sailor is a man of adventure, and
Hudson was all of that. In those days the most
sought-after things came from the East—Asia
and the Indies. But it often took as long as two
years for a sailing ship to go from Hudson's native England to this land of treasure, and return.

The sailor's dream was a shorter route. Many had tried to find it, among them Jean Verrazano, Henry Cabot, Christopher Columbus. Hudson's particular dream was that the quick route could be found to the northeast, through cold icy seas and over the North Pole. Twice he persuaded an English company to send him off in a ship on this dangerous route. Twice he was forced to turn back. He begged the directors of the company to give him another chance. They refused.

But Hudson was a determined dreamer. He wrote to Henri IV, the King of France, offering his services to that nation for the same daring experiment. The King said "No!"

In 1609 the Dutch were the richest commercial nation on the globe. Every year their shipyards turned out a thousand vessels to fetch and carry goods to and from all ports. They were more eager than any other nation to find a quick way to the Indies. They had organized a company for this very trade, the Dutch East India Company.

Early in 1609 Hudson appeared before the directors of this company. There was fire in his eyes. He was making a bid for his last chance to follow his star of fortune.

"Gentlemen," he said, "give me a ship! Give me a crew! I will bring you back a cargo of gold—of elephant tusks—of nutmeg and pepper —of sweet perfume—in one-third the time it takes now."

There was much shaking of heads.

"We have sent four expeditions your way," said one graybeard. "DeMouceron, Barentsen, Cornelissen and Heemskerck have all come back. They found only ice."

"But I will crash through the ice," said Hudson. "Beyond it lies the open sea and the way to Asia."

He remained in Amsterdam for days, renewing his plea. The Dutch, being persistent, admired persistence.

Finally one day he was summoned before the directors again. He faced them excitedly.

"Do I go?" he asked.

"We can pay you only eight hundred guilders," said one cautious director.

Three hundred dollars to seek the world's greatest goal!

"Where is my ship?" said Hudson.

Then Peter Plantius, a kindly clergyman on the board, added:

"And if you don't come back, we will pay eighty guilders to your wife!"

Thirty-two dollars for a husband lost!

It is doubtful whether Henry Hudson heard, he was so eager to be on his way.

They gave him an awkward, clumsy brig with two masts and square sails. Away he sailed— an Englishman under the Dutch flag. There are some who say he was being untrue to his native land by sailing under another flag. But an adventurer of Hudson's zeal knows no native land. He was being true to his dream.

However, his dream was not true to him. Again he came upon ice, great mountains of

The Half Moon's *prow was turned toward America*

it, forbidding and impenetrable. His crew, used to sailing in the soft, blue, warm southern waters, rose in rebellion. He was forced to turn back.

He did not wish to confess failure, so he turned to another's dream instead of his own. Verrazano had been sure there was a route to Asia through the American continent which Columbus had discovered. Hudson turned the *Half Moon's* prow toward America.

It was thus that on September 12, 1609, skirting the shores of our continent, he came upon the fabulous harbor that is now New York

Bay. Manhattan Island gleamed in the sunlight, and several strange, dark, semi-naked men wearing head feathers waved to him from the shore and then put out in bark canoes to greet him.

2

RED MEN AND WHITE

THE natives who paddled out, not so much to greet as to inspect these strange white men and their great "canoe" were, of course, the first Americans—the Indians.

They were tall, broad of shoulder and keen-eyed. Their skin was the color of cinnamon, a brown that in the bright sunlight seemed almost red. They were, in fact, called red men by the first strangers to this shore.

These Indians lived on Manhattan Island and the nearby mainland, but not in permanent towns or cities. They were nomads, roamers. Their homes were huts called wigwams. These were built by placing two rows of upright saplings opposite each other, bringing the tops together, covering them with boughs, and lining the inside with bark.

Wigwams were kept warm in cold weather by fires built on the floor. The smoke escaped from a small hole at the top, for they had no windows.

There were large wigwams and small ones. Several families could live in a large one because an Indian needed only room enough to lie down straight at night.

The men hunted and fished. The women raised the crops, did the planting and the plowing and the cooking. Some of the dishes have come down to us, notably succotash, a mixture of beans and corn. In fact, the Indians were the first to cultivate corn. Another of their crops was tobacco. They eventually taught the white man to smoke tobacco. But no one realized it would turn into a billion-dollar business.

The Indians used shells for money, which

Indians paddled out to inspect the strange white men and their great "canoe"

they called wampum. The purple lining of the mussel shell, cut in small cylindrical shapes, was worth twice as much as the white conch shell. They wouldn't take gold as a gift. It wasn't the right color.

More valuable than wampum, however, were the odd trinkets the sailors traded for the furs and copper and oysters and corn the Indians brought out in their canoes. Hudson's men paid them with stockings, which the Indians used for tobacco pouches, and axes and shoes which they hung about their necks for ornaments.

But the greatest demand was for beads and buttons. These brought such fancy prices in traded articles that they were to rule the American market in days to come. This great Manhattan Island was later to be bought from the red men for twenty-four dollars' worth of buttons and beads.

There is every evidence that at the start the Indians were friendly. They paddled out to greet the *Half Moon* with no fear. Hudson sent a party ashore the next day and the Indians received them with no sign of enmity. A little later Hudson himself was entertained by a chief and his family. He was served, as a treat, roast dog—a somewhat doubtful delicacy. When Hudson declined to spend the night in the wigwam "palace," the chief believed the refusal was due to fear. This so upset him that he broke his arrows and threw them into the fire.

One unfortunate incident did occur. A group of the *Half Moon's* seamen were sent to find out how deep was the approach to the island. They encountered a canoe filled with Indians. Suddenly the sailors were showered with arrows. One struck an Englishman named John Coleman in the neck and killed him.

No one knows why the Indians attacked the sailors. They made no effort to capture the sailor's boat, or even to follow up the first volley, so it may have been fear. Anyway, the first blood had been shed. Coleman was buried on land near by called then, and now, Coleman's Point.

The harm had been done. Later there was to be more bloodshed.

Hudson, now distrusting the natives, made ready to move on. This island was beautiful. But after all, the great wide river, the biggest he had ever seen, must be the way through this continent to the Orient and the fulfillment of his dream.

He moved cautiously up the river, dependent on the wind that was needed to fill the sails. On September 23rd, after about ten days of slow progress, the small boat which had been sent a few leagues ahead to make tests of the river's depth, reported:

"Seven foot and unconstant soundings!"

Hudson was near the present site of Albany and could go no farther.

His bubble had burst again. This river was not the path to Oriental treasure. Sadly he turned back. His men were tired and discouraged now. So was he. He took to the ocean, and on November 7th he arrived at Dartmouth, England. Here another blow awaited him. The English authorities seized him. He had, they said, no right to enter into the services of a foreign power.

The *Half Moon,* on the demand of the Dutch government, was returned to Holland some months later. So was Hudson's report, a glowing account of the river and the beautiful land he had found. But his report was tinged with a note of disappointment at his failure to fulfill his real mission.

The Dutch East India Company was disappointed, too. But money was still pouring in from the East. The company had little interest in the small trickle that might come from the West.

However, two shrewd sea captains did see beyond their Dutch noses. They were looking one day at the furs the *Half Moon* had brought back.

"They're as fine as any I've ever seen," said Captain Adriaen Block.

"They're as good as those I just brought back from Russia," said Captain Hendrick Christiaansen.

Then they looked at each other.

Furs were much worn in the cold countries of Europe. They came from Russia. The Netherlands alone sent a hundred ships a year to Archangel. But the Czar had issued a new decree. It imposed a heavy tax which made furs more expensive for the Dutch to buy.

Captain Block made inquiry.

"Hudson's men tell me these Indians in the New World know nothing of taxes, and will trade furs for belt buckles and such," he told Christiaansen.

A month later the two captains had char-

The Tiger *caught fire while lying off Manhattan*

tered a ship and were on their way. They came
back with a great cargo of fine pelts. They
brought back two real live Indians, too, feathers and all, and exhibited them throughout the
Netherlands. People flocked to see the red men,
and to buy furs.

Three rich merchants put up the money for
two bigger ships, the *Fortune* and the *Tiger*.
American trade had started in earnest.

One night in November, 1613, the *Tiger*
caught fire while lying off Manhattan and
burned to the water's edge. Captain Block and
his crew escaped to shore. Captain Christiaansen

and the *Fortune* had just sailed back to Holland and would not return until spring.

There was nothing for those marooned on shore to do but build a new boat. Block and his sailors had no tools, but they made crude ones of copper, stone and shells. The Indians fed the white men and helped them. Considering the difficulties, building the boat was a monumental task. But these Dutchmen were equal to it.

By spring the new ship was launched. It was called the *Restless* and it was more than just seaworthy. It was a triumph.

While all this was going on, Captain Block and his men had to live ashore. The huts they built were the first homes of the white man on Manhattan Island. Later Manhattan was to house millions of men and women.

3

THE INDIANS SELL AN ISLAND

IF Peter Stuyvesant had not changed his mind about becoming a sailor, he probably would have reached the island in whose history he was to play an important part much earlier than he did. But wooden guns replaced wooden ships in his games and the ambition to be a soldier triumphed over his seafaring dreams.

Soldiers were the heroes of the day in the old Netherlands, their glory achieved in the newly won freedom from Spain. But sailors were still far more important to New Netherland. For that was the name now given to the fur-trading base across the ocean in America.

The Dutch authorities were eager to encourage exploration which might lead to new fields of trade. So they had passed a law providing that "Whosoever shall, from this time forward, discover any new passages, havens, lands or places, shall have the exclusive right of navigating to the same for four voyages."

Captain Block, arriving home with a shipload of beaver skins in October, 1614, heard of this new law. He rushed before the States-General, the body of men that ruled the Netherlands, claiming the exclusive right to trade with America.

"But Henry Hudson discovered the river and the island of which you speak," said Jan van Olden Barneveldt, the great Dutch statesman.

"Yes," said Block, "but I have discovered a new passage which opens up new lands."

The elders looked skeptical.

"My sailors will bear me out," insisted Block.

They did, for Block, nosing about in his homemade ship for more Indians from whom to buy more furs, had crashed through a strait so dangerous it was later to be known as Hell Gate.

"And I came upon a beautiful inland sea," he told the elders, "extending eastward to the ocean."

This was Long Island Sound.

For finding it, the States-General gave Block and his partner, Christiaansen, a four-voyage trade monopoly. It was in this grant that the land was first referred to as New Netherland.

It was not long afterward that the term "New England" appeared for the first time officially. Captain John Smith, whom Pocahontas had rescued somewhat dramatically, had used the term to describe land he had explored in what is now Maine and Massachusetts. In 1620 King James I let it be known that he had determined to grant a patent "for the more northerly parts of America, distinct from the Virginia patent, and to be called by another name, to wit, New England."

Where were the boundaries of these two new territories? No one seemed to know. Without question they overlapped. Later each was to claim ground the other held. It was to be a long and troublesome argument for many years, and it was to plague Peter Stuyvesant when he became an important figure in the new land.

Meanwhile the fur trade went on. It took Captain Block's ships three years to complete their four voyages, and before they were completed a vast new scheme had arisen to engulf New Netherland. Dutch eyes were looking west at last. The East Indies were still the source of wealth, to be sure; but there were West Indies, too. If the Dutch East India Company, which controlled the trade in the East, had paid its shareholders 425 percent profit, why not have a company to control trade in the West?

And so in 1621 the Dutch West India Company was formed. Probably no private corporation was ever granted such power. First of all, it was guaranteed the trade of the Atlantic Ocean shores of Africa and America—not just North America but South America, too. It could appoint and discharge governors, administer justice, wage wars.

The company didn't bother much about New Netherland at the start. It had other stakes. It set out to vanquish and humble the Spaniards. Its ships, commanded by Admiral Piet Heyn,

Cows, as well as people, came to New Netherland in 1625

captured a Spanish fleet, freighted with silver intended to replenish the Spanish treasury. Heyn also seized other ships with rich cargoes worth almost $5,000,000.

Dutch soldiers took most of the West Indies, including Curaçao, much of Brazil, and San Salvador. Their exploits thrilled all of Holland.

It was at this time that young Peter Stuyvesant decided to become a soldier.

"But I wanted you to be a man of God," said his father.

"I will serve God in the army," said Peter.

"Wait," said Dominie Stuyvesant. Peter consented to go to college, and to wait. But his mind was not on his studies.

So stunning were the Dutch victories in South America that North America was neglected. But the company had promised to colonize the lands its charter embraced. Therefore, in 1624, the ship *New Netherland* brought thirty families with all their hopes and ambitions to the new land. The newcomers went at their tasks eagerly. That first year the income from the fur trade jumped to 28,000 guilders.

The directors of the Dutch West India Company opened at least one eye. They would build a town upon this island. They called for volunteers. Who wanted to settle in America?

Six families—forty-five persons—came over in 1625. And what was almost as important, 103 cows, pigs and sheep. New Netherland began to resemble a permanent settlement.

Then the Dutch sent over a governor, Peter Minuit. He was so sure this colony was here to stay that he called the Indians together and, in 1626, bought Manhattan Island legally and properly.

He paid twenty-four dollars for the 14,000 acres, not in money, but in beads and buttons and other trinkets. It turned out to be a great bargain. It wasn't a bad deal for the Indians, either. They were not cheated, as might appear in the light of what happened afterward. The value of the land depended entirely on the use made of it. The Indians didn't need it. They had plenty of other land on which to hunt, and that's all they wanted to do. They hadn't invested a cent in the land. The twenty-four dollars was clear profit.

4

THE FORT BECOMES A COLONY

IT was Governor Minuit who really planted the Dutch flag on American soil, for he built a fort from which it could fly. It wasn't much of a fort, to be sure, just a crude blockhouse. Nor did it yet have any soldiers. It was named Fort Amsterdam, and not long afterward the little community took on the name of New Amsterdam, after the great city in Holland.

There were about thirty thatched huts now,

and a horsemill, the upper room of which was set aside for religious services. There was no clergyman as yet, but there was a *krankenbe-soecker,* a consoler of the sick. He read the Scriptures to the small congregation every Sunday.

And there was, from the start, great religious freedom. Walloons, Huguenots, Calvinists, Quakers, Catholics and Jews were to live happily together and worship freely, even in the early days of what was eventually to be the most cosmopolitan city in a big world.

Governor Minuit wrote a friendly letter to Governor Bradford at Plymouth and received a friendly reply. But before the exchange of correspondence was over, a testy tone had crept in, with each warning the other to respect boundaries. What boundaries, neither could be sure, but this was the beginning of a dispute which was to be long and bitter.

The Dutch began to realize that occupation would be nine parts of possession, which is, of course, nine points of the law. They sought new ways to populate their colony.

In those days there were three classes in Holland: the noble landowning families, the burghers who controlled city life, and the common people. The burghers were ambitious to become landowners but Holland was small and there was no land to be bought.

The Dutch West India Company set up an alluring plan for the burghers in America. Any stockholder in the company who would plant a colony of fifty people could acquire a plot of land sixteen miles in length on one side of the river, or eight miles on both. He was to be called a patroon, and he would become to all intents and purposes a feudal lord, with the right to make laws, establish courts, and leave his title to his heir. He would be subject only to the States-General, the ruling body of Holland.

Not a few of these domains were established. One was near the site of Albany, and belonged to Kiliaen van Rensselaer, a wealthy jeweler of Amsterdam. It was to become a severe thorn in the side of New Amsterdam. It was responsible for the recall of Governor Minuit, who was no doubt jealous of it. And Patroon Van Rensselaer was able, through his influence, to have appointed in Minuit's place as governor, a thoroughly incompetent gentleman named

Wouter van Twiller, who had married Van Rensselaer's niece.

Van Twiller was good-natured, even though incapable. He had the energy that sometimes characterizes the mediocre. He brought with him 104 soldiers, so he felt he had to fix up the fort. This was a much needed improvement. He brought with him also a minister, Dominie Everardus Bogardus; so he built a new church. It was a structure of dubious architectural merit, but built on the end of the island where it could be seen by all, including ships at sea.

However, the church was of little use to Van Twiller. No sooner was it up and in use, than he had words with Dominie Bogardus, a strong-minded character who did not approve of the Governor's lax administration. Bogardus denounced him from the pulpit as "a child of the devil." The Governor swore never to enter the church again—and he didn't.

Van Twiller also brought with him the colony's first schoolteacher, Adam Roelandsen. But he didn't build him a school. The legend is that the teacher had so little to do, and got so little for it, that he took in washing!

The Governor built windmills in New Amsterdam

The Governor also built three windmills. Nor were they much help, because he built them so close to the walls of the fort that they didn't catch any wind. He also established a cemetery.

Van Twiller wasn't a forceful character. He exchanged letters with Governor Winthrop of Massachusetts Colony about the constantly recurring question of English-Dutch boundaries. But his letters lacked authority.

One day an English vessel named the *William* sailed into the harbor. It was commanded by Jacob Elkins, a Dutchman who had been discharged by the West India Company, and who had entered the service of the English. He announced his intention to trade with the Indians.

Van Twiller told him he couldn't. Elkins said the territory had been discovered by an Englishman, Henry Hudson, and he could.

Van Twiller ran up the Dutch flag on the fort and fired three shots over the *William*. Elkins ran up the English flag on his ship and fired three shots over the fort. Then he calmly sailed the *William* up the river in bold defiance.

The Governor was in a rage. He summoned the entire populace into the fort, opened a cask of wine and a keg of beer.

"Drink!" he commanded. "Drink to the confusion of the English!"

The good citizens drank, but the English were not confused. By this time they were on their way to Albany.

It happened that New Amsterdam had a distinguished visitor at the moment, Captain David Pietersen deVries. He was a swashbuckling hero of many adventures at sea, who was later to colonize Staten Island. That day he was Van Twiller's guest at dinner. The incident came up.

"If I had been governor," said Captain DeVries, "I should have given him a helping of eight-pound iron beans! Right now I'd send a ship after him and drive him out of the river!"

The slow-witted Van Twiller thought this over. He decided DeVries was right. So he sent a shipload of soldiers after Elkins. They found him near Albany trading for furs. They made him give up the furs, and sent him down the river, out into the ocean, and no mistake about it.

Van Twiller enjoyed this display of authority so much that a few days later, when DeVries ordered his own ship through Hell Gate for a trading voyage, the Governor forbade the sailing and trained the guns of the fort on the ship.

"The country is full of fools," De Vries shouted at him. "You let the Englishman through when he violated your river, and you try to stop me when I don't."

The Governor sent twelve soldiers down to deal with this defiance; but DeVries jumped in his small boat, rowed away, and left the soldiers to be laughed at by the crowd.

However, Van Twiller wasn't a complete fool. He acquired in his own name, not that of the company, a great deal of valuable property. This included two of the best farms in Manhattan, the river islands now known as Welfare and Governor's Islands, a plantation at Red Hook, and a large tract on Long Island. He soon became the richest man in the colony.

A gentleman with the highly improbable name of Lubbertus van Dincklagen, the *schout-fiscal,* or sheriff, became suspicious of all this wealth. He reported it to the States-General in Holland. When Van Twiller heard about it, he discharged the sheriff and shipped him back to Holland. This was a mistake. Van Dincklagen was thus able to present his case in person.

As a result, Van Twiller was recalled. But not until his Governor's Island farm was stocked with all the fine cattle in the colony. Van Twiller said they had all just wandered there. But it was strange that previously the cattle had done their wandering on Manhattan, and hadn't ventured into the channel that separated Manhattan from Governor's Island.

5

SHADOWS ON THE NEW LAND

THERE had been talk in Holland of sending a military man to rule New Netherland. But the best military men were reserved for the colonies where fighting was as important as trading. For this reason, South American colonies still got the better governors.

It was true that the British colony to the north of New Netherland kept expanding and, with each expansion, further encroached on the lands claimed by the Dutch. These settlers were becoming more and more belligerent, too. It would seem that only the fact that the British had to worry about a possible civil war at home in England kept them from encouraging the colonists and causing real trouble for New Netherland.

Just about this time, too, the Swedes had planted a colony on the shores of Delaware Bay to the south. The Dutch saw this as a new threat and it was, for the Swedes were pretty determined to stay and to get their share of the New World's trade. Moreover, they had a great name as a warring nation.

The Indians were also becoming more restless and resistant. They were fighters and were not always treated fairly, so they sometimes fought unfairly. But one of the few real accomplishments of the muddle-headed Van Twiller was a peace treaty he concluded with the two most belligerent tribes. This happened just before his "reign" ended. So with these friendly relations established, the military aspect of the governorship became less important.

Peter Stuyvesant might have heard the earlier army talk about Fort Amsterdam and New Netherland, because he did hold to his decision to become a soldier. He graduated from the university, as he had promised his father, but he convinced the old dominie that he wasn't meant to be a minister.

He joined the army. But it wasn't all that he had hoped it would be. He didn't mind the military life. He rather enjoyed it. However, he didn't like to take orders. He was happy so long as he could give them, but to reach that position in the army meant a long wait. He wasn't prepared to wait that long, so he resigned. He was still looking for adventure, though.

So it happened that about the time that the directors of the Dutch West India Company were quietly looking for a man for a big job, Peter Stuyvesant applied to them for a little job. He was put to work as a clerk in the office of the company.

But Peter was meant for bigger things. He had his eye on something more exciting and it wasn't long before he got it. In the fall of 1635 he sailed for Brazil, a real land of adventure. Now he was a supercargo, the officer in charge of cargo and commercial affairs, and he was giving orders in a small way.

Work in the colonies meant fighting, too, and here Peter's army experience proved invaluable. There was no question about his ability, his sagacity, his bravery. With each new responsibility he proved himself ready for more until, in 1643, he was appointed acting Governor of the Island of Curaçao. However, that's a few years ahead of our story.

When Wouter Van Twiller was recalled as Governor of New Netherland in 1637, things had calmed a bit and no military man was needed for the post. The colonists, however, hoped for a good strong leader. They felt sure they could not do any worse than Van Twiller. They were wrong.

It was as though the authorities in Holland had tried to choose the most unworthy candidate. They selected a man who had gone bankrupt as a merchant. According to Dutch custom his portrait had therefore been nailed to the gallows. That wasn't exactly a mark of distinction!

To make it worse there were dark rumors concerning him. Not long before, he had been provided with money and sent on a mission to Turkey to ransom Christian captives. The rumors were that he had kept the money for his

Peter as a clerk for the Dutch West India Company

own uses, and left the captives in their captivity.

His name was Wilhelm Kieft. And it is not to be wondered at that there was no welcoming committee to greet him when he arrived in March, 1638, in the good ship *Herring*. He was a bustling, bristling little man and he immedi-

ately took all the power unto himself and proceeded to rule in the manner of a tyrant. He
had little judgment, and was irritable and quick-
tempered.

Things were not going well in New Netherland and might have gone even worse. However, at this point the directors of the West
India Company decided to make a new effort
to develop the colony.

This time the company offered free passage,
and as much land as a person could cultivate,
to anyone willing to settle down. The settlers
had to pay only a quit-rent of a tenth of what
they produced. Complete religious freedom also
was promised, and the promise was kept.

Colonists—men and women of better stock—
began to arrive. The settlement expanded. It
branched out to Long Island and New Jersey.
David deVries, who had gone back to Holland
in disgust a few years before, returned now with
some friends and founded a colony on Staten Island.

Farms—*bouweries* they were called in Dutch
—flourished on every side. New Amsterdam itself was beginning to look like a town. Thatched

cottages with wooden chimneys began to sprout. Lots sold for about fourteen dollars. Compared with today's values in New York the figure seems enviably small. But it was really quite large. Remember, the whole island had been bought only a few years before for twenty-four dollars. The town had a bakery and a brewery and a village green, where the people danced and bowled on holidays.

Paths and lanes began to grow into streets: Beaver Street, Wall Street, Pearl Street, Stone Street. Most of them still exist in downtown New York today and are about as narrow as the original paths.

The widest of the streets and the one that did the most twisting and turning was called Heere Straat, or Main Street. Later its name was to change to Breede Weg—in English, Broadway, which it is called today. It is probably the most famous street in the world. Martin Krieger was the first grantee of a lot on Breede Weg, and here he erected one of the town's first taverns. Its location, at the beginning of Broadway with a bright lantern over its doorway, was prophetic. It was the beginning of the "Gay White Way."

Dominie Bogardus' parsonage was a lovely little house, perhaps the prettiest in the village, with a garden filled with gay flowers. He even grew love apples. They were green plants with large bulbous fruit that turned red. No one ate them in those days because they were considered poison. We eat them today. We call them tomatoes.

But the dominie needed a new church. There were no funds to build one. The way Governor Kieft raised the money for the purpose is a good example of how his crafty mind worked. At this opportune time a daughter of Dominie Bogardus was married. All the prominent and wealthy citizens of the community were invited. The wine flowed freely. Everyone was merry.

When good spirits of both kinds were at their height, the wily Kieft passed the subscription paper for the new church. The good citizens vied with each other in their pledges. The next morning they were not quite so public-spirited, but they had signed their names. Kieft collected every penny from them and the church was built. It was named for the good St. Nicholas, the man who in our own Christmas legends became Santa Claus.

With all the good things that were happening
—new blood and new building—the colony
should have abounded in happiness. But there
were shadows, heavy shadows, upon the growing
settlement. From the south, the Swedes were
moving gradually northward in open challenge
to the Dutch. From the north, the English were
moving steadily and defiantly southward.

The greatest shadow was far more sinister. The
Indians were angry because of the injustices they
had suffered. Inflamed by the liquor the white
man gave them, and armed not with primitive

Dominie Bogardus grew love apples

bows and arrows but with firearms for which they paid dearly in beaver skins, the red men were becoming more and more restless. They were sullen and brooding—and they were cruel, tricky fighters. Trouble was in the air.

6

THE INDIANS STRIKE BACK

THERE were Indians on every side of the Dutch: Mohicans, Mohawks, Raritans, Tanka-tikes, Weckquaesgeeks, Hackensacks and Canar-sies, to name a few of the most prominent tribes.

They evidently wanted to be friends from the moment they paddled out in their canoes to greet Henry Hudson. There is no doubt that with wise and just treatment they would have worked hand in hand with the white man. They traded with him happily, they gave him food and taught him how to grow and use the native crops.

But traders in those early days almost always became greedy sooner or later. This was the cause of almost all the early Indian wars. The Dutch wanted to get as many furs as possible to send back to Europe. They made every effort to entrench themselves with the bronze trappers. They invited them into the fort, and plied them with "fire water" which made them quarrelsome. They allowed them to become familiar with the inadequate defense of the colony. Worst of all, they introduced the Indians to firearms.

The savages had at the start looked upon guns as "devils," and would not use them. They clung to their tomahawks and scalping knives. These were much more vicious implements of warfare, but much less effective. The Indians found that out in their first few skirmishes with the invaders.

Soon guns and gunpowder were the most coveted medium of exchange. So eager were the Indians to get the white man's weapons that they would trade as many as twenty beaver skins for one gun. Unscrupulous traders took advantage of this.

The colonists at Rensselaerwyck were particularly guilty on this count. The result was that the Mohawks, whose hunting-grounds bordered on their lands, became the best armed of the tribes, and before very long were exacting tribute from the other tribes.

In New Amsterdam a law was proclaimed forbidding the sale of firearms to Indians, so the Algonquins and other nearby tribes got none. That made them angry at what seemed discrimination in favor of the Mohawks.

At this point, in 1640, Governor Kieft bobbed up with a stroke of bad administration that was almost a work of genius. The settlement was short of provisions, so he decided to levy a tribute of corn on the Indians. His excuse was that they owed this for the "protection" the Dutch gave them against their enemies.

The chief of the Mohicans sent word to Kieft:

"You and your brothers came to our land uninvited. We gave you beaver skins for everything we got from you. We gave you food when you needed it. We helped you build a ship and kept you alive while you were doing it. We taught you to grow our crops. And now you want to take part of our corn for nothing."

But Kieft would not listen. By this time he had worked up an antagonism against the red men. He was looking for any excuse to quarrel with them, largely because he felt he could conquer them.

Badgered at every turn, accused of stealing everything that was missing, the Indians were in no mood to be friendly. They took every occasion to be offended. They recalled every forgotten injustice. They revived all old grudges.

One of these grudges had to do with an incident that had occurred some ten years before among the Weckquaesgeeks. An Indian and his nephew, on their way to New Amsterdam with furs, had been attacked by some Dutch freeholders. Their furs had been stolen and the older Indian killed. The boy had escaped. He vowed revenge.

Now in this atmosphere of suspicion and accusation, his brooding mounted. In August of 1641, he traveled to New Amsterdam and went to the first house he saw, that of Claes Smits, the wheelwright. The Indian offered a beaver skin for trade. When Smits turned to find some woolen cloth to offer for it, the Indian killed him with one blow of an ax.

Governor Kieft saw this as an excuse to over-power the Indians. He demanded the murderer from his tribesmen. They refused to surrender him. Kieft was all for war. But he sensed a lack of approval from the community. Because the *bouweries* were scattered, without much defense, he decided not to take the full responsibility.

So in 1641 he called together the heads of families. It was the first popular assembly held in the colony.

The voices of those who wanted the war were the loudest. But there were other voices.

"It is all right for you who are secure in a good fort to want war," shouted Gerrit Adraen-son. "You haven't slept a night away from it since you've been here."

"How do we know," demanded Hendrick van der Horst, "that you do not want to divert atten-tion from your accounts which may have irregu-larities?"

Finally the meeting selected twelve men to weigh the evidence and make the decision. The twelve deliberated at length and ruled that the Governor should again demand the surrender of the murderer. If the request was again refused, revenge should be sought "with proper regard to

God and the opportunity." Peace should be preserved if possible, but if war could not be avoided, "Governor Kieft should lead the van."

Kieft was far from pleased. He called the twelve men together again. But instead of discussing war against the Indians, they demanded reforms in government, including a true voice in the affairs of the colony which Kieft ruled as a dictator. Kieft ordered them to meet no more.

Now the colony was in a turmoil. There was a war party, headed by Kieft and the colonial secretary, Cornelis van Tienhoven. There was also a peace party, whose leaders were Captain De-Vries and Dominie Bogardus.

The good dominie was so worked up that he denounced Kieft from the pulpit. Whereupon the Governor not only absented himself from church every Sunday, but gave orders to the fort's garrison to conduct maneuvers outside the church during the sermon, accompanied by the beating of drums and the firing of cannon. However, the dominie was not only determined but loud, and succeeded in being heard.

Finally the Governor managed one of his characteristic tricks.

At a Shrovetide feast at the home of Jan

The dominie denounced Kieft from the pulpit

Jansen Damen when all were merry with wine, Van Tienhoven presented a petition which purported to speak for the twelve men. It urged Kieft to avenge the death of Smits by an instant attack on the defenseless Indians.

Drinking a toast to the success of the venture, Kieft hastily ordered his soldiers to attack.

Hearing of the action, both DeVries and Bogardus rushed to the Governor. They begged him to hold off.

"The order has gone forth," said Kieft. "It cannot be recalled."

At midnight, February 25, 1643, the soldiers came upon a peaceful Indian village near Pavonia. Without warning they struck. Those who were not murdered while asleep in their wigwams sought to swim the river. Many drowned—a few escaped. Some fled to the Governor's house for refuge.

"The Mohawks have fallen upon us," they cried. "Let us hide ourselves in the fort."

DeVries, who was still trying to plead with Kieft, told them:

"No Indians have done this deed. It was the Dutch. Run for the woods."

And he helped them escape.

That night there was another Indian massacre at Corlaer's Hook. Women and children were

A peaceful Indian village was set on fire

not spared. The Indians fled in terror—those of them who lived to escape. Their cries were heard for many miles. Then all was quiet.

The victory was celebrated in silence in New Amsterdam. There was an air of foreboding for several days. Then again the cries of the Indians were heard. This time, though, they were war cries.

Eleven tribes rose against the Dutch. They attacked not only with the white man's guns but also with their own tomahawks. The fields, the swamps, the morasses were filled with wild-eyed red men. The Dutch were shot down working in their fields, their cattle were driven off, their houses were burned, their women and children were carried into captivity. The peaceful countryside became a shambles. Rich farms were laid waste, fences torn down, crops and trees uprooted. No one was safe outside the fort.

Our wars with the Indians were seldom conflicts in which to take pride. This one was particularly inglorious because it had its beginnings in deep injustice. That the Indians might have been made useful, happy neighbors was shown by an incident at the height of the war. DeVries' settlement on Staten Island was surrounded and set on fire. Suddenly one of the Indians saw De-Vries and raised his hand.

"Stop!" he told the attackers. "This is the home of our friend!"

The fire was put out. The Indians withdrew. The man who saved DeVries, it turned out, was one whom DeVries had saved the night of the massacre at Pavonia.

The ambush war went on for two years. Heads could not be seen without shots being fired.

But two thousand miles away on a little island in the West Indies other shots were being fired which played an even more important part in the story of New Amsterdam and Peter Stuyvesant.

7

WE MEET PETER

PETER STUYVESANT knew what was going on in New Netherland. As Governor of Curaçao —his province included Aruba, Buen Aire and other small islands of the Leeward group off Venezuela—his reign had been for the most part peaceful. But he knew that a fellow governor, Kieft, was having his troubles. When the Portuguese scored a victory over the Dutch in Brazil, more than a hundred escaping Dutch soldiers landed in Curaçao. Things were so quiet there they were not needed, so Stuyvesant sent them on to Kieft, who did need them badly.

Curaçao's chief product was salt, which Stuyvesant sent back to Holland in great quantities. But life in the hot, inactive colony was pretty dull.

It isn't any wonder that a man as enterprising as Stuyvesant was ready for adventure. Even a rumor was enough to stir his patriotic spirit, if it meant excitement. One such rumor came ashore with a shipload of sailors. It spread swiftly. The Portuguese, who had been having considerable success in Brazil, were planning to take Curaçao!

Stuyvesant, in the manner of modern warfare, planned a counter-blow to throw the enemy off balance before the attack. He would lead an expedition against the island of St. Martin. It would serve a double purpose, for his soldiers could relieve a Dutch colony which was being besieged there, and it would set the advancing foe back on his heels.

Stuyvesant was in his element. He planned his expedition carefully. He asked for and was given a day of "fasting and prayer to obtain a blessing" on his expedition.

On January 14, 1643, he and his men set out in the good ship *Blaewe Hoen*. They reached St. Martin without trouble. Stuyvesant led his men ashore. Suddenly there was a burst of fire. Stuyvesant kept going but his soldiers did not. They had been fighting in Brazil. They were tired. They didn't care whether they took St. Martin or not. It wasn't a very attractive island.

So they ran.

A few of them stopped and turned back, for they saw that their leader had fallen. They carried Peter Stuyvesant aboard the ship. His right leg was shattered. They took him back to Curaçao.

From his bed of dejection and pain Peter ordered a number of his soldiers discharged.

"It is difficult to catch hares with unwilling dogs," he lamented.

Peter reported the incident in a letter to his employers in Holland.

"Honorable, wise, prudent and most considerate Lords, whose welfare and prosperous government may thrive," he began, rather elaborately.

"My last letter was sent by Mr. Renandt in March last, by which I advised your Excellencies of my intended attack on (the isle of) St. Martin, which however did not take such effect as I had hoped for, the handicap—and not a small one—being the loss of my right leg, which was shot off by a cannonball.

"After a 28 days' siege we proceeded from St. Martin to Curaçao, where we learnt of the evacuation of Maranhoan for want of victuals and also that the Commander Wiltschut with some 450 souls had arrived there. These circumstances caused me pain, much misery and difficulties, finally resulting in a serious illness, from which God only may give deliverance. This however is why I cannot pay my respects to your Excellencies in such a form and style as I should have wished, which your Excellencies in their customary wisdom may excuse."

The little doctor at Curaçao tried desperately to mend the shattered leg, but he couldn't. So he amputated it. It was buried on the island, and Peter felt for a time that he had been buried with it for he was discouraged and ill. The pain kept on. Amputees will tell you that a missing leg will seem to remain long after it is gone. So it was with this one. Finally the little doctor said there was nothing more he could do.

Peter knew that the finest surgeons in the world were in his homeland. Indeed, in the little town of Leyden there was a great medical university. He asked the Dutch West India Company whether he could go home for treatment. The answer was "yes." He sailed back in the ship *Milk Maid.*

Imagine Stuyvesant's surprise, when he landed in Holland, to find himself in the very good graces of the Dutch West India Company.

There was a good reason for this. Things were not going well with the company. The conquests in Brazil had ended. The tide was going the other way. The company was almost bankrupt. It was trying to hang on to what it had.

Peter was summoned by the directors when he arrived. Still weak and unhappy, he trembled a bit. But the directors greeted him with smiles and warm handshakes.

"Congratulations!" one shouted.

"You saved Curaçao," said another. "The Portuguese have not attacked. You frightened them off."

Peter was summoned by the directors of the West India Company

Peter began to smile.

"It was true Roman courage," said another director.

Peter patted his wounded leg. This praise almost made losing it worth while.

"Never mind," said the director general. "You shall have the best of medical care."

"You shall have a new leg—the best guilders can buy."

"And when you are well and strong you can have your governorship back. We need men like you."

They cheered as Peter left the room. His spirits soared.

Stuyvesant went to Leyden, where the company retained the best of doctors for him. He spent some weeks there under their care. They finished the work the little doctor in Curaçao had started. But they said he could not go back to his post at once.

When time came for him to convalesce he went to the home of his sister, Anneke, in the nearby town of Alphen-on-Rhine. While he was away she had married Samuel Bayard, son of a French Protestant minister who was a refugee from his native land.

It was good to be back in Holland again. It was spring and the tulips were just beginning to bloom. Peter sat in the warm sunshine and watched two storks building a nest on his sister's roof.

Soon he was ready for his new leg. It wasn't just an ordinary wooden leg. That wouldn't have been enough for Peter Stuyvesant. This was a wooden leg with great silver bands on it. Indeed, so much of it was covered with silver that the legend grew it was composed entirely of silver. "Old Silver Leg," they called Peter in his later years.

It wasn't easy to walk on it when he tried. However, he had help. All through his recuperation there had been a frequent visitor at the Bayard house. She had fair hair, she was young, she was charming. She came ostensibly to see her brother, for she was Judith, Samuel Bayard's sister.

But she stayed often to talk to Peter, or to play the spinet for him, for she knew music well and loved it.

She was helpful, too. Peter was impatient. He wanted to be in action. He would storm at the slowness of his recovery.

"Now, Peter," Judith would say. "You can't order nature around. Just wait until your leg heals."

When the new leg came and he tried to walk fast and stumbled, he would let loose a torrent of strong Dutch words.

"Now, Peter," Judith would say. "You'll just have to get used to it slowly."

"But I have work to do," he would shout.

"It will wait."

In Holland Peter began to convalesce

And she would walk with him along the canals and through the lovely gardens.

Then one day he asked her to walk with him always, and she said she would.

8

PETER TAKES OVER

JUDITH and Peter were married on August 13, 1645, in the little church at Breda. In this little town her father had enjoyed the freedom of worship which had been denied him in France.

Judith made a stunning bride in the gay wedding dress of the Dutch ceremony, her many colored petticoats, and the little jeweled crown which was handed down in her family from bride to bride.

Peter was a handsome bridegroom with a coat of soft velvet trimmed with lace, diamond buttons, and gold buckles. Shining brighter than anything else, however, was his silver-banded leg, which had become a symbol of strength instead of weakness. He could stand upon it with dignity and he could stamp upon it in anger. It was to become as much a part of him as if it were flesh and blood.

As his strength returned so did his confidence and ambition. He went to Amsterdam to tell the directors of the West India Company that he was ready for service again.

His post in Curaçao had never been permanently filled. Things had not been going well for the Dutch in the West Indies, and not much effort was made to keep these colonies in good shape. What was worse, the colony of New Netherland was being allowed to disintegrate. It might easily have slipped out of the hands of the Dutch at this time, for they were in no mood to hold it and had little money to spend for the things that it needed.

However, it now was becoming increasingly evident that if the Dutch didn't want this territory, the British did. They kept edging down from the north, with covetous eyes on Long Island and Manhattan. The Dutch reacted as most humans do. If someone wants something you have, you are persuaded it must be valuable and you decide you want it yourself.

So it was with New Netherland. Bankrupt and discouraged though they were, the directors of the company began to feel that this struggling colony in the New World must, after all, be an asset. How could they hold it? They must find a strong man to place at the head of the colony. He must have both military and executive experience. He must be loyal to the company, for it must be remembered that this was a private enterprise.

Where would they find the man for this difficult job?

The answer clumped into their directors' meeting one day on a silver leg. It was Peter, of course, although he could not have guessed that he had arrived at the opportune moment.

"I am ready, sirs," he told the directors, "to return to my post."

He meant, of course, Curaçao. The directors looked him over and found him practically as good as new. They told him they would consider his case. Some weeks later they sent for him. They told him that he had been reappointed governor of the Curaçao colony.

"Thank you, your High Mightinesses," he sputtered, "I will endeavor——"

But before he could finish, the company's spokesman went on to say that he also was to be governor of the province of New Netherland.

Peter was stunned. But he was not abashed. He knew his strength. He felt sure that he could fill this new post successfully, although he knew it would not be an easy task. He was grateful for the opportunity; and in that gratitude was born immediately a loyalty to the company which had given him the opportunity. This intense loyalty was to cause many of his troubles.

But there was no thought of troubles as he took the oath of his office in July, 1646. In fact, things had taken a turn for the better in New Netherland. Peace had been made with the Indians. There was no need to hurry to New Netherland, so it was five months before Peter set out for his post.

Finally on Christmas Day, 1646, he and Judith boarded the ship *Princess* in Texel Harbor. There were three other ships in the little fleet—

the *Raet,* the *Great Gerrit* and the *Zwol*—for it was a large expedition.

The company sent with Peter a new council: Lubbertus van Dincklagen, Vice-Director; Hendrik van Dyck, *Schout-Fiscal,* a sort of sheriff and prosecuting attorney combined; Adriaen Keyser, Commissary; Jessner Thomas; and Captain Bryan Newton, an Englishman who had served with Stuyvesant in Curaçao.

Peter's sister, Anneke, decided to try her fortune in the new land too, and took her three sons with her. In addition, there were servants, a company of soldiers, and a large group of adventure-seekers who are always willing to seek new thrills, if not fame and fortune, in a new land.

Peter must have felt very proud as he stood on the bridge of the *Princess* and led the little fleet out of the harbor.

There is evidence that he felt a little too proud. First of all, he ordered the expedition to proceed to New Amsterdam by way of Curaçao. No one seems to know why. It may have been a personal whim. There were protests. Evidently Peter had determined to prove he was the commander. It was a rough voyage. Some of the passengers died or were lost overboard. But Peter held firm.

Near the Caribbean the fleet fell in with a Spanish vessel whose papers did not satisfy Stuyvesant. He seized the ship as a prize. While he was in his cabin trying to decide what to do with the vessel, *Schout-Fiscal* Van Dyck dropped in to offer his advice.

"Get out," shouted Peter. "When I want you I will call you."

Van Dyck reminded Peter that such legal matters were part of his duties, but Peter roared him out of the cabin. Later, when the fleet lay under the scorching tropical sun in the harbor, the Governor and all the others visited the port, but Van Dyck was not even allowed "a stroll ashore."

All this would seem to indicate that Peter knew his task was a big one and that he was trying to prove to himself that he was ready for it —that he was master.

It was May 27, 1647, when the fleet sailed into the harbor of New Amsterdam. The heartiness of Peter's welcome was unmistakable. At the fort the very last ammunition on the island was

*On Christmas Day four ships left Holland bound for
New Netherland*

used in firing a joyful salute. On the banks of the East River every man, woman and child of the colony stood cheering and beaming.

The new Governor and his party came ashore. They made their way through the happy burghers to the fort. There a few of them became unhappy because, it was reported, the Governor kept them waiting "for several hours bareheaded" while he was covered "as if he were the Czar of Muscovy."

But all in all it was a happy throng looking forward to good government at last.

The crafty Kieft, hoping to take advantage of this warm glow, leaped to his feet to make a sentimental speech of farewell. He thanked the burghers for their fidelity to him. But the burghers were too smart for him.

"We have no thanks for you," they shouted angrily. The roar of the crowd increased. It was getting out of hand.

Then Peter Stuyvesant stepped forward. His very bearing commanded silence.

"I have come to bring justice for all," he said. "I will govern you as a father his children."

There was quiet. Peter had taken over.

9

PETER AND JUDITH TAKE A WALK

PETER looked again to be sure. He had just awakened on his first morning in New Amsterdam, and was standing at the window in his old-fashioned nightshirt and tasseled nightcap. He stretched as he peered out at the grounds within the fort.

Peering back at him was a cow. That's why he looked again. But there it was—and a moment later a goat stepped alongside and stared, too.

The governor's house, in which he had taken

residence, was inside the fort. The ramparts of the fort were earth covered with sod. The animals—and there were many more—were grazing on these ramparts, which had crumbled in many places and were no longer much of a protection.

Peter called Judith to look, too. She laughed.

"It is no laughing matter," said Peter. "Suppose they were Indians?"

Judith shuddered. She had heard of Indians.

"We must have the ramparts repaired, and made of stone," Peter said.

He and his wife dressed. When they sat down to breakfast there was a bowl of yellow porridge in front of each of them.

"What's this?" demanded Peter.

"*Suppawn,* sir," said the servant. Before the Stuyvesants could ask any more questions he went on. "It's Indian corn, ground and mixed with milk."

Peter and Judith tried it cautiously, and promptly finished the bowl. They were to learn to like corn in many ways.

It was a bright, warm day, and Peter was eager to have a look at his "domain."

"We shall walk through the town," he told Judith.

As they stepped out of the governor's house arm in arm, Peter was smiling. But almost immediately the faint trace of a frown crossed his face. For he saw that the fort was in very sorry condition. Then the Stuyvesants passed the church. It had never been completed. Peter frowned again.

Peter and Judith went out into the streets. They could hardly be called streets. They were little more than country lanes or roads, and they were thick with dust. It was obvious that a shower would turn them into mud bogs.

The burghers smiled and bowed to the Stuyvesants from their front doors. Peter did not always bow back. He was looking at the houses, wooden structures with wooden chimneys sticking out of thatched roofs.

"A spark would set any one of them on fire," said Peter. "And a wind would carry the fire to the others and burn everything. This must be remedied."

Pigs and goats wandered aimlessly. Garbage was thrown everywhere. The whole place was neither beautiful nor fragrant. Peter was muttering to himself. Judith was holding his arm now and patting it to calm him.

"Where is the schoolhouse?" Peter asked a passerby.

"Oh, we have no schoolhouse," was the reply.

"No schoolhouse!" echoed Peter testily, and stamped on.

Finally he and Judith stopped at a corner in front of a tavern. Voices could be heard inside. Peter eavesdropped for a moment, hoping he might hear what his burghers were talking about.

What he heard was profanity and rowdy laughter. He straightened. At this moment a figure came through the door. It was an Indian, and he was intoxicated. He lurched dangerously near

An intoxicated Indian staggered from the tavern

Judith. She clung to Peter. He took her arm and hurried her away.

As they walked back to the governor's house Peter stormed. With each step his temper mounted. Instead of clinging to his arm, Judith now patted it.

"Patience, Peter," she said. "All in good time."

But Peter was not a patient man. The next morning he was up with the sun. He set about organizing his council. To the men he had brought with him he added several who were already on the ground and were familiar with the situation. He chose well. His councilmen were not yes-men, as Peter was eventually to find out. They were staunch citizens with the best interests of the community at heart.

In this respect Peter was like them, for he had fallen in love with this new home.

He called the council together at once and they set to work. From that moment proclamations came booming from the Governor's office with the noisy authority of shots from the fort's cannon.

The first proclamation on record dealt with the Sabbath. It must be respected by all. Workmen were employed at once to repair the church, and Stuyvesant immediately joined the congregation and set an example of regular and devout worship.

Drunkenness and brawling were made offenses, and a court of judgment was established.

Selling of liquor and firearms to the Indians was forbidden.

The fort walls were repaired.

The crooked, winding paths were straightened and became streets. Volunteers cleaned up the rubbish and the garbage and dumped it into the bay. Citizens were ordered to build fences to contain the roaming goats and cows, and to hide their unsightly and far-from-aromatic pigpens and chicken coops.

The Governor appointed a commission of three to regulate the erection of new buildings and to see that the owners of vacant lots kept them properly.

The fire hazard was dealt with vigorously. Three fire wardens were named to inspect all homes. Owners of chimneys found to be dangerous were fined three guilders. If a house was burned through an owner's carelessness he was fined twenty-five guilders.

When Peter sought to solve the problem of an adequate school he ran into a complicated situation. Money had been raised to build a school but had been diverted to various pressing debts, such as pay for the fort's soldiers.

This discovery led Peter to inquire into the colony's finances. What he learned was somewhat disturbing. It developed, on the one hand, that unscrupulous traders were smuggling out furs to be sold in Virginia and New England. Conversely other traders, equally disloyal, were smuggling goods into the colony without proper payment.

Stuyvesant promptly established a spot near the guns of the fort where inbound and outbound vessels were required to anchor for supervision. Thus lost revenues were retrieved.

Soon the burghers of New Amsterdam began to smile again. Peter made friends immediately with the neighboring Indian tribes, and won their confidence. They literally "buried the hatchet," a ceremony symbolic of peace.

The misgovernment of Kieft had shaken the faith of those he governed. Now the burghers saw their little town emerging from the shadows. Peter Stuyvesant really seemed to be keeping his promise to rule them as a father his children. New Amsterdam began to take on a warm and comfortable glow. It began to expand. It became a pleasant place in which to live.

10

LIFE IN NEW AMSTERDAM

"THIS country suits me exceedingly well," wrote Nicasius de Sille from New Amsterdam to friends in old Amsterdam. "I shall not try to leave it as long as I live.

"It goes here after the manner of the Old Testament. Wealth consists in oxen and goats. Children and pigs multiply rapidly and more than anything else.

"The soil is good. The rivers are full of fish.

Oysters we pick up before our fort. The weeds consist mostly of strawberries, catnip and blackberries. The Indians supply us with venison, wild geese, turkeys, partridges, ducks, wild pigeons and other birds. Beer is brewed here as good as in Holland. Wheaten bread is more common than rye or buckwheat. Oats, peas and corn are fair.

"The women of the neighborhood entertain themselves with pipe and brazier. Young and old they all smoke. In fine, one can live here and forget the fatherland."

Governor Stuyvesant was responsible for this new feeling of security and well-being. Life, after many trials and fears and discouragements, was good in this growing colony. There was strength in the fortress now—not only newly buttressed walls but strength of character.

These happy days began for the burghers at the first break of day when Gabriel Carpsey, the cowherd, blew three loud blasts on his horn. Then he started his rounds to gather the cows of the village and take them out to pasture.

Moments later, smoke would begin to curl from each chimney as the housewives, called *huys-vrouws,* began preparing breakfast. From that moment on there was always smoke to be seen, if not from chimneys, then from long pipes which almost every Dutchman smoked. These men of the town would be followed through the day by their smoke. The older and wealthier burghers traded furs or lumber. The younger ones chopped wood, or threshed grain, or ground it in the mill, or fished.

The women kept their houses shining clean. They could be found knitting, spinning, or weaving almost constantly, for families in those early days could not be clothed properly without clicking needles or whirring wheels in each household. Theirs was the job, too, of tending the little gardens that went with every house. The vegetable garden included corn and other foods to which the Indians had introduced the newcomers. In the herb garden they grew herbs not only for seasoning but also for medicines. And every house had a gay flower garden.

Always there were tulips to remind them of the fatherland—and pinks, roses, marigolds, violets, anemones, and also blooms known as gillyflowers, jenoffelins and faredames. Then there

Tulips reminded them of the fatherland

were the flowers native to this new land—sunflowers, morning stars, red and yellow lilies.

Everybody worked until almost sunset, when the herdsman brought the cows home to be milked. Then there usually was a visiting hour during which neighbors sat on the little benches at the door of every home and exchanged the day's news and gossip, the men nodding and smoking.

After that, there was supper—not dinner, for that was in the middle of the day—and perhaps a quiet hour spent sitting in front of the hearthstone while *mynheer* had his final pipeful. And then to bed. If it was cold, a warming pan made the chilly sheets comfortable, and there was a thick feather-bed to snuggle under. Then curfew and "tap toes" from the fort—and silence.

The burghers could hear, if they could keep awake, the steady footsteps of the *kloppermann,* or rattle watch, as he walked through the streets. They could hear his rattle, which he sounded now and then to prove he was there. And they could hear his voice as he called out each hour and the weather.

Then at the break of day would be heard the herdsman's horn and the watchman's voice:

"A fair morning and all's well."

So began another day.

With the reforms Peter instituted because of fire hazards, the town began to take on the appearance of most villages back in old Amsterdam. Many of the houses were of brick, with high tiled roofs. The windows were small because glass had to be brought from Holland and came in small pieces. The doors were divided in half—one could open either the upper or lower part, or both. Doors like that are still used in this country and they are called Dutch doors. The farmhouses were especially well built but spread out over more ground than is the custom today.

Early Dutch houses were famous particularly for three places: the garret, the cellar and the kitchen.

The garret was at the top of the house, its ceiling slanted because it was formed by the roof. It was the storehouse. Into it went castoff furniture, trunks, bandboxes, outgrown cribs and cradles. The windows were dingy, there were spider webs, and it had a musty smell. The garret's only practical use was as a drying place for clothes on a rainy washday. And it was a great place for the youngsters to discover discarded oddments which had been put away and forgotten.

The cellar was a world apart. It was built to be warm in winter and cool in summer. In it were great bins which held potatoes, apples, turnips and parsnips. On shelves were great cheeses; from the ceiling hung hams and sides of bacon and necklaces of sausages. There were hogsheads of corned beef and barrels of salt pork. There were barrels of pickles and vinegar and cider, and kegs of pickled pigs' feet. There were jars of preserved fruit. And there was, above all, an aroma provided by all these things which was indescribably wonderful.

The kitchen was the busiest room in the house. It fairly bustled from morning to night. It was dominated by a high, wide fireplace, at one side of which stood the great brick oven for all baking. There was a turning spit for roasting meats. Across the chimney was a back-bar from which hung pots and kettles at varying heights above the fire. Sometimes these chimneys were wide enough to drive a horse through. The fireplace always was large enough to roast a whole pig.

All week long the fireplace and the oven were busy. The fires never went out but were just banked at night. On Sunday, though, there was no cooking. The family dressed in its Sunday best—and so did the fireplace. A curtain or petticoat of homespun linen, red or blue, was drawn across it on a string. It rested, too.

The parlor was the *sanctum sanctorum,* Washington Irving tells us. The mistress of the house and her domestic, if she had one, spent many hours keeping it clean. But no one else was allowed to enter it except on rare and unusual occasions. Its handsome fireplace was lined with beautiful blue Delft tiles from the Netherlands, usually depicting Biblical scenes.

There were no carpets in the days of the Dutch. Indeed, the famous (or infamous) Captain Kidd was the first householder on Manhattan Island to own a carpet, and that was not until some years later. In the early Dutch days, the floors were swept with a thin layer of sand, and then this sand was brushed into decorative shapes and left on the floor.

The bedrooms were distinctive for one object, the *bedstee*. This was a bedstead built right into the wall, usually with two berths, as in a Pullman. In the daytime these were hidden by doors which were closed.

The dining room was gay and cheerful. There was always a cupboard, and there was beautiful silver brought or sent from home, fine porcelain for which Holland was famous, stoneware, china, and pewter polished to the point where it shone like silver.

And there was food. The Dutch women knew how to cook, the Dutch men loved to eat. The result was a boon to all of us, for down through the ages have come recipes that are almost legendary. These are the real Dutch treats.

Life was earnest, life was real in these early

days of Manhattan, but it was also pleasant. Almost everyone went to church, but Sabbath observance was not so strict as in New England. Although dancing and fishing and games were forbidden and the tavern bars closed, the day was one not only of worship but of rest and relaxation. Once a burgher was arrested for having an ax on his shoulder on Sunday, and he escaped with no punishment when he proved he intended only to fashion a toy bat for his son.

The Dutch were a blithesome people. All of their holidays were happy ones. Christmas was their great holiday, and they brought Santa Claus to us in the form of their jolly St. Nicholas. He was the patron saint of this colony, and the first church in New Amsterdam was named for him. The Dutch also gave us the Easter custom of coloring eggs. And they brought to our shore that happy custom of the New Year's Day call, a custom now almost forgotten.

The social life was simple but gay. In the winter there were sleighing parties that wound up at homes on the outskirts where hot chocolate was the strongest beverage served. In the summer there were rowing parties to Breuckelen, which, as you probably have guessed, was what today is known as Brooklyn.

There was bowling on the Bowling Green. It still is the Bowling Green in downtown New York, but without bowling. There were wonderful walks down Maiden Lane, which still is called Maiden Lane although it is now a business street. There were rides across the Tamkill, a little stream emptying into the East River. There were rides over the Kissing Bridge, too, so named because it was permissible while crossing it to salute your feminine companion with a kiss.

So life in New Amsterdam was hearty and happy.

Peter and Judith entered into this life as leaders of the community should. Their state dinners were simple but had a definite dignity. They took an interest in the social life of the burghers, but there was never any mistaking that they were the Governor and the Governor's wife.

Their own life was a happy one. In 1647 their first son was born, named Balthazar for his grandfather. A little more than a year later came a second son, called Nicholas after the patron saint of the colony.

The colony was booming. Its burdens were becoming lighter. Its place in the world was becoming bigger.

Peter should have "reigned" joyously over his thriving subjects. But he didn't.

11

PETER MAKES A MISTAKE

PETER STUYVESANT'S sun had just begun
to shine on New Netherland when a cloud appeared. It was the first of many which were to
bring shadows to what should have been bright
days.

Peter's was a complex personality. He was a
man of warm affections. But he was also a man
of prejudices and passions. It must be remembered that he came to New Netherland as a mil-

itary governor. He was, essentially, a military man, and as such he expected that his authority was not to be questioned.

Most of the citizens of New Amsterdam were so happy to be free from the rule of the unpopular Governor Kieft that they were willing to let his reckless administration be forgotten. But two of them asserted their right to speak out. Jochem Kuyter and Cornelis Melyn, both good citizens, had suffered considerable losses because of Kieft's misrule. They were not content to let matters drop.

So they presented to Governor Stuyvesant and his council formal accusations against Kieft. They demanded an investigation into his conduct in office, starting with his foolhardy attitude toward the Indians which had led to a bloody war.

To Peter, the military man, this amounted to mutiny. No soldier must question the actions of a general whether these are right or wrong. Kieft had been the governor. Therefore to Peter his conduct was above criticism.

It was an unreasonable attitude but Peter undoubtedly felt that if these men were allowed to question Kieft's conduct, they might even one day question his.

He called a meeting of the council immediately. But he didn't even wait for the members to gather before he denounced Kuyter and Melyn in no uncertain terms.

"Disturbers of the public peace and tranquility!" he stormed.

Peter did not give his councilmen a chance to speak their minds. He spoke his.

"If this point is conceded," he shouted, "will not these cunning fellows claim even greater authority against ourselves, should it happen that our administration may not square in every respect with their whims?"

"But perhaps they have cause to ask——" began Adriaen Keyser haltingly.

Peter stopped him with a bang of the gavel.

"It is treason," he roared, "to petition against one's magistrates, whether there is cause or not."

No one had the courage to argue with this imperious voice. The petition of the two men was rejected.

The decision emboldened Kieft. He saw an opportunity to clear his badly besmirched name and a chance to achieve personal revenge against his accusers. He took advantage of Stuyvesant's loyalty to his office, and tried to lead the colony to believe it was a vindication for himself.

Taking the offensive, Kieft trumped up charges against Kuyter and Melyn. He accused them of stirring up much of the trouble of which they accused him.

Kuyter and Melyn answered these charges in a straightforward manner, but by this time Peter was thoroughly aroused. At his orders the two were arrested for "rebellion and sedition."

Their trial took place almost immediately. There were no lawyers in New Amsterdam and so they defended themselves. They submitted ample proof of their charges against Kieft and complete justification for their action in questioning his administration.

But they didn't have a chance. Peter had appointed himself judge and had prejudged the case before it began. He heard the evidence without listening. The two men were pronounced guilty.

Melyn was banished from the colony for seven years and fined three hundred guilders. Kuyter was exiled for three years and fined one hun-

dred and fifty guilders. Peter had been determined on death sentences, but Judith, always a
restraining influence, prevailed upon him to be
lenient.

"We will appeal to the States-General," said
Melyn when he heard the sentence.

"This is forbidden," shouted Peter from the
bench.

The prisoners were silent.

"If I were persuaded that you would bring
this matter before their High Mightinesses," the
Governor continued, "I would have you hanged
on the highest tree in New Netherland!"

This attitude was Peter's first mistake. The
decision was extremely unpopular. There was
much muttering in the taverns. Peter had lost
much of what he had gained. But he remained
stubborn. At the mere mention of the subject he
flew into a fury and "the foam hung on his
beard."

There were whispers that some of the burghers might carry an appeal to the fatherland.

"If any one during my administration shall
appeal," Peter barked, "I will make him a foot
shorter and send the pieces to Holland and let
him appeal in this way."

Instead of winning vindication through the trial, Kieft found that he was more unpopular than ever. People turned up their noses when they met him in the street.

Now it so happened that a ship named the *Princess* was to sail soon to return Dominie Bogardus, the retiring shepherd of the little flock, to Holland. Kieft took advantage of this opportunity to escape from his unpleasant situation. He, too, booked passage, taking with him, so his enemies said, 400,000 guilders in ill-gotten gains. The exiled Kuyter and Melyn sailed also, but as prisoners.

When the *Princess* was well on her way, tragedy overtook her. She was driven by a storm into the British Channel and wrecked off the rugged coast of Wales. She began breaking up. At this point Kieft's conscience at last caught up with him. Turning to Kuyter and Melyn, he pleaded:

"Friends, I have been unjust toward you. Can you forgive me?"

Before he could get his answer, a wave swept him overboard and he was never seen again. His enemies said that this was retribution—a bad end for a bad man. But Dominie Bogardus was also drowned, and he was a good man.

A wave had swept Kieft overboard

In the midst of all the horror and confusion, Kuyter had a strange experience. He found himself on deck standing next to another man. At least he thought it was a man from what he was able to make out in the murky light. Just then a portion of the decking broke. Kuyter spoke to his unknown companion but received no answer. It was only then that he discovered it was a cannon! Realizing it would sink the wreckage, he quickly got off and managed to swim ashore. The cannon was washed up later and erected by the Welsh as a memorial to the eighty who died in the shipwreck.

Melyn was among those saved. For days he

and Kuyter searched the shore for a box which contained their papers. Finally they found it.

Word went back to New Netherland of the wrecking of the *Princess*. The story was that all aboard had been lost. Peter said it served Kuyter and Melyn right. He shed no tears. But when they presented themselves in Holland to press their case, he must have felt that their ghosts had risen from the ocean. In any case it was not they but his first mistake that haunted him. He was to make others that were to torment and trouble him in the days to come.

12

THE BURGHERS DEMAND A VOICE

NOT all of Peter's mistakes were his own fault. His was not an easy task. The very nature of his position made things extremely difficult for any but the most skillful diplomat. This Peter was not. He was a good administrator, a man of great courage, but he was neither subtle nor artful.

His greatest problem was one which was almost impossible to solve, for it was one of conflicting loyalties. It was to torment Peter all the days of his rule.

Peter's subjects in the New World, the Dutch-men who had left home to dig in here, were tough-fibered. They were fighters by nature. They had fought the seas and they had fought the Spaniards. They were the most adventurous members of a fighting breed.

These settlers in a new land had been used to political liberty at home. There they had been ruled by the States-General, the governing body of a progressive nation, Holland.

Here in America it was an entirely different story. They were ruled here by a private organ-ization—the West India Company. Peter had been appointed not by the States-General but by the directors of this private company. He was a man of intense loyalty, and by his code his loyalty belonged to his employers.

Peter's ability as a governor brought peace and prosperity to the colony almost immediately. He had a way with the Indians. He used author-ity and just treatment and charm, and the men-ace of threatened attack vanished. The ravages of the war with the Indians disappeared. Trade grew. The community thrived.

However, with all of these strides forward, the burghers became more restless and discontented. They were restless to begin with. Only the restless emigrate from a country as prosperous as Holland was in those days.

To Stuyvesant, a government consisted of a governor and those he governed. He had been appointed governor, and no one must question his authority. But the people wanted to be part of the government, as they had been at home. They wanted to elect their representatives.

Here Peter's loyalties clashed. He had to be faithful to the West India Company which employed him, and the company did not concede that the people had any rights in its affairs. But Peter knew in his heart that taxation without representation was not right.

How could he give the people representation without really giving in and allowing them to elect men to office?

Finally he worked out a compromise. The people would elect eighteen men, from whom he and his council would select nine to "advise" them—three merchants, three burghers, and three farmers. Six of these were to be replaced, each year thereafter, by six chosen from twelve elected by the people.

This somewhat complicated system gave Peter a chance to save his face and yet to make a gesture to the people.

The Nine Men went to work happily—at the start. They cooperated in repairing the fort and in making other improvements. However, this happy state did not last long. By the time the second group of Nine Men was chosen, there was an open clash.

The people now wanted a greater share in the government. They wanted really to elect their officers and to make decisions. This time Peter's temper flared. What did these cobblers and millers and tavern-keepers know about governing? What training had they had to compare with his? And how could they help make laws? They were always breaking them, so far as he could see.

All this might have been worked out amicably with diplomacy. But there was no diplomacy here. The Nine Men decided a delegation must be sent to the Netherlands to present the demands of the people to the States-General.

The first Peter heard of this was when the

Nine Men requested him to call a meeting of the burghers with the intention of asking them to finance this trip. Peter's shouts could have been heard for miles.

"No!" he stormed. "There will be no meeting. If you want to communicate with their High Mightinesses, you must do so through me. I will decide what protest is to be made to them."

The Nine Men knew what that meant. So they decided to teach Peter a lesson. There was no one among them disposed to smooth the ruffled feathers of this angry peacock.

Instead, refused the right to hold a meeting, they went from house to house, asking each resident for his moral support and for financial help, too. Adriaan van der Donck, secretary to the Nine Men, took down these interviews. The plan was to read them to the authorities in the Netherlands.

When Peter heard that this was being done, he peg-legged it in person to Van der Donck's house, walked in without so much as knocking, and seized all the papers. He dismissed Van der Donck from his post as secretary to the Nine Men and threw him into jail.

Van der Donck was thrown into jail

It was at this tense moment that one of the
ghosts that had risen from the wreck of the *Princess* returned to haunt Peter. Cornelis Melyn
arrived on a ship from Holland. He had in his
possession a mysterious paper bearing the seal
of the States-General. There were many whispers
as to what it contained.

Melyn was determined to wipe out the dishonor of his banishment at the hands of Stuyvesant. He called a meeting of the burghers in
the church one starry night in 1649. Peter found

out about it. Just as Arnoldus Hardenburg rose
and began reading aloud the document Melyn
had brought from Holland, Peter stalked into the
church.

"Stop!" he commanded.

Hardenburg kept on reading.

Enraged beyond control, Peter rushed at him.
He clutched at the paper. Hardenburg held on to
it, and tried to go on reading. A struggle ensued. Burghers, taking sides, joined in the melee.

Finally the seal was torn from the paper and
fell to the floor.

The fighting stopped at once. Peter was so-
bered. He had great respect for the law and all of
its symbols. This seal was a symbol of Holland's
government.

Hardenburg recovered the paper, smoothed it
out, and began reading aloud.

The document was a compete vindication of
Melyn and Kuyter. It was also an official dis-
approval of Peter's conduct in their case.

Peter listened, his head bowed. The meeting
ended. The crowd filed out. Peter felt the sting
of this official rebuke and, what hurt even more,
his defeat at the hands of the people.

13

THE ENGLISH EYE NEW NETHERLAND

AFTER that episode Peter could no longer prevent the people from sending a delegation to the homeland to present their case.

They raised the money to pay for the trip, and they prepared their case carefully. In charge of this phase of the work was an old antagonist, Adriaan van der Donck. Peter, in his remorse, had freed him from prison.

Van der Donck was an adversary worthy of the name. A graduate of the University of Leyden, and not only a learned man but also an enlightened one, he was the first lawyer to settle in New Netherland. He was patient where Peter was impetuous. He was reasonable where Peter was short-tempered.

If Peter had worked with Van der Donck instead of against him, his part in the history of New Netherland might have been even more important. For Van der Donck loved this new country in the same way that Peter did, and he had a great feeling for the democratic principles which were to make it free and great.

But Peter was smarting under defeat. He was proud, and his pride had been hurt. It would have been wise of him to join the growing movement for liberty. But his resentment forced him into an opposing position.

He, too, sent a delegation to Holland, a one-man delegation. But he chose the wrong man: Cornelis van Tienhoven, a crafty politician who shared Peter's resentment with even greater bitterness, for he had quarreled with almost all the men who led the movement. Van Tienhoven was keen-witted and eloquent but he was not always honest, and he would use any means to achieve his end.

Van der Donck prepared his case for the people in the form of a history of the colony. This story (for it was really that rather than a document) was called *Remonstrance of New Netherland to the States-General of United Netherland.* That's not a very interesting title, but, just as Van der Donck is an unsung hero, it is an unsung classic.

The part that these early Dutch settlers played in the slow but never-ending struggle for liberty is not always appreciated. But in Van der Donck's book it shone forth. When Van der Donck and his fellow-delegates arrived in Holland, they had the history published. It was widely read and helped their case. immensely.

Referring to the book's popularity, the directors of the West India Company had this to say in their next letter to Stuyvesant:

"The name of New Netherland was scarcely ever mentioned before and now it would seem as if heaven and earth were interested in it."

But in spite of this surge of interest in the colony, Van Tienhoven was able to prolong the fight for freedom. He asked for postponement after postponement. He indulged in all the delaying tactics he could invent. But the delegation hung on. Weary months passed and still there was no decision.

Meanwhile Peter had new worries at home. The burghers themselves, while restless, were not unruly. Of course Peter, still resentful, lost his temper now and then and behaved somewhat childishly. He found out that *Schout-Fiscal* Van Dyck had aligned himself with his opponents. Peter promptly removed him from office, and humiliated him by giving him the job of keeping the pigs out of the fort.

However, in spite of his pettiness, Peter could rise to an occasion when any threat arose to these people with whom he quarreled but whom he nevertheless loved. And there was a threat.

From the north, the frontiers of the English kept advancing on the little Dutch province. There was trouble brewing and Peter knew it.

The English had looked with eager eyes on New Netherland even before they settled in America. The Pilgrims, when they left England to seek religious freedom, went first to Holland where they found it. But they were eager to go on to what William Bradford, one of their number, called "those vast and unpeopled countries of America which are fruitful and fit for habitation." They asked the Dutch for ships, and expressed the hope that they could settle in the Dutch colony here.

But the Dutch weren't sure they wanted their land colonized by Englishmen. The States-General decided against giving the Pilgrims ships.

Bradford and the others who were determined to cross the ocean then accepted the English offer to go to the Virginia colony. They set sail in

Van Dyck keeping pigs out of the fort

the *Mayflower* in 1620. We all know what happened, and how they landed in Plymouth.

But there is evidence in the log of the *Mayflower* that these Pilgrims had hoped to land nearer the Dutch colony and were greatly disappointed when they didn't.

Bradford himself wrote that they resolved to set sail again and "stand for the southward, to find someplace about Hudson's River." However, the danger of rounding what is now Cape Cod deterred them, and they finally decided to settle where they had landed.

All during the years that followed, the English cast envious and covetous eyes on New Netherland. They constantly moved southward. Now the English territory and the Dutch began to overlap. Disputes arose from time to time. Friction grew until, under Stuyvesant, it became a real and aggravating problem.

14

PETER TRIES FOR PEACE

FROM the day he became governor, Peter tried
to settle the disputes with the English amicably.

The Dutch had an honest title to the land.
But they wanted it largely as a territory in which
to trap animals for furs, or to buy furs from the
Indians. They didn't want to settle down and
farm.

The English, on the other hand, said the land
was too good to stand idle in this way. They

moved in and planted crops. Soon their farms and villages were everywhere. Hartford and New Haven grew into good-sized settlements.

Stuyvesant saw some justice in their feeling about the land, but again he was committed to his company and to its claims. He wrote to Governor Winthrop of Massachusetts, hoping to arrange a meeting to talk things over. Winthrop was willing, because the people of his state were not near enough to New Netherland to care deeply about it one way or another. But Governor Eaton of New Haven, whose people were moving in on Dutch territory rapidly, persuaded Winthrop to delay. So the Governor of Massachusetts wrote Peter that he would meet him when his health permitted.

Peter tried again and again to arrange a meeting with Winthrop. The answer was always the same.

"Any man who is that sick," stormed Peter when he finally lost patience, "must be dying or lying."

Always dramatic, Peter waited for a chance to go into action, which he knew would do more than words to bring about a settlement.

One day news came to him that a Dutch ship,

the *Saint Benino,* was taking a cargo into New Haven. Now New Haven, on Stuyvesant's map, was in New Netherland and yet the ship's captain was paying no duty to the Dutch government. This was enough for Peter. He pronounced the *Saint Benino* a smuggler.

It happened too that the deputy governor of New Haven had just bought a ship, the *Zwol,* in New Amsterdam, and it was about to be delivered to him. But Peter seized it, put a party of soldiers aboard the ship, and sent it into New Haven harbor on "the Lord's Day." It anchored alongside the *Saint Benino.* Suddenly the soldiers leaped from the *Zwol* to the *Saint Benino,* captured it and its crew, and sailed it back to New Amsterdam.

Peter had done what he wanted to do. He had stirred up a hornet's nest. And the maddest hornet was Governor Eaton. Even Governor Winthrop suddenly became well enough to protest.

Peter really wanted to settle the boundary problem. He felt that there could be no real peace in America until it was settled. So he persuaded the New England authorities to name two delegates to a conference. Realizing it would be

The Dutch and English discussed boundary lines

easier to negotiate a settlement if language was not a barrier, he named two English citizens of New Netherland—Thomas Willett and George Baxter—as the Dutch delegates.

The meeting was to be held in Hartford. It took Peter and his delegates four days to journey there. All along the way they saw English farms and villages. It was clear to Peter, once again the fair-minded Peter, that the English had a real claim to this territory. They were cultivating it and improving it. They cherished it. This gave him much to think about.

But Peter was not ready to admit too much. The first paper he submitted to the conference was headed "Hartford in New Netherland." Immediately there was a storm that almost swamped the meeting.

However, when he and the other delegates settled down to their deliberations, they made an earnest effort to work out a fair boundary line.

In this atmosphere the arbiters arrived at their solution:

"That upon Long Island, a line run from the westernmost part of the Oyster Bay, so and in a straight and direct line to the sea, shall be the bounds betwixt the English and Dutch there; the easterly part to belong to the English, the westernmost part to the Dutch, the bounds upon the mainland to begin at the west side of Greenwich Bay, being about four miles from Stamford, and so to run a northerly line twenty miles up into the country, and after, as it shall be agreed by the two governments of the Dutch and of New Haven; provided the said line come not within ten miles of Hudson's River."

The delegates, warmed by their peaceful achievement, urged "a nearer union of friendship and amity" between the English and the Dutch.

But when Peter took his news back to New Netherland, he got neither friendship nor amity from his own peoples. Actually, no matter what the result had been, the Dutch wouldn't have liked it. But that Peter had given away land, even land they didn't use or particularly want, infuriated them.

Nor did it help that Peter's negotiators at Hartford had been English New Netherlanders.

The burghers protested vigorously to the Dutch government at home.

"We have surrendered more territory than might have formed fifty colonies!" they wrote indignantly.

As a result, Holland's ratification of the new boundaries was delayed for years.

But the burghers were wrong and Peter was right. The treaty, had it been officially confirmed at that time, would have meant English recognition of the Dutch rights to New Netherland. No longer could the English have claimed the colony they later seized on the pretext that it was their own. If Peter had had his way, the Dutch might still be in New York today.

15

THE TOWN BECOMES A CITY

WHILE the people in New Netherland were grumbling without very much to grumble about, the delegates who had gone to Holland to fight for a greater share in their government were patiently carrying on. Days dragged into weeks and weeks into months.

The West India Company did everything it could to create vexatious delays. It had a wily advocate at court in the shrewd and unscrupulous Van Tienhoven. He tried to paint the burghers who had signed the petition as selfish men seeking advantages for themselves rather than the freedom of the many.

It was not easy for the delegates to stay in Holland through this long siege. The West India Company hoped they would get discouraged and go home. But they were determined. And the people in New Netherland kept sending them funds to live on.

Finally the time came when no more obstacles could be thrown in the way. Their "High Mightinesses" in the States-General handed down their decision.

New Netherland was to have a "burgher government," a government in which its citizens were to have an active part. It was to be ruled by two burgomasters, or mayors; a *schout,* or sheriff; and five *schepens,* or aldermen. And they were to be elected by the people!

There was great rejoicing in New Amsterdam, but this happiness did not extend to Peter. For along with this decision of the States-General came an order. He was to return to Holland and give an account of his administration.

By the same boat came a contradicting order from his employers, the West India Company. He was to stay where he was until further notice.

Here was Peter, again torn between two masters.

Events settled the issue for him!

There had been a revolution in England. Charles I had lost his head. Oliver Cromwell had come into power. He was as jealous of the Dutch as his predecessor. It did not help that the Prince of Wales and the Duke of York had fled to Holland. They were Stuarts, of course, and enemies of Cromwell.

Finally, the fire that had smoldered for so long broke into flames. War was declared between England and the Netherlands in July, 1652.

Peter threw back his shoulders when he heard the news.

"Now we must watch the North!" he said. "We must repair the fort. We must be ready!"

Immediately he became the soldier again. And the States-General, back in Holland, recognized his value now. They acted at once. They withdrew the order for his recall. Not

Peter launched a campaign of preparedness

only was he to stay on, but he was to launch an immediate but quiet campaign of preparedness. However, he was not to do anything to upset his neighbors, now really enemies, to the North.

As a military leader, Peter became a new man. He rose to the occasion magnificently and he worked with his people, and they with him, in the face of danger.

One of the very first things he did was to call a meeting. He presented the problem of what the war might mean to New Netherland. The citizens agreed that a number of them should mount guard every night at the fort. They agreed, too, that the fort should be put in a proper state of defense, and they decided to enclose the city by a ditch and palisades. Work started at once, and no one worked harder than Peter.

There sprang up a fine feeling of warmth between the Governor and the governed. Quarrels were forgotten. Pettiness and pride disappeared.

Then as the year 1653 began in this pleasant glow, there came an official announcement from the Governor.

New Amsterdam was proclaimed a city!

This was a new gift to the people and one they didn't expect. Peter's detractors said it was not he but the officials in Holland who granted this new honor to New Amsterdam. But Peter's letters to the States-General, revealed later, prove that it was he who suggested the distinction.

The ceremony took place on February second, the day of the feast of Candlemas. The official bell ringer—he was called the *klink*—led the procession from the fort to the church. Then followed Governor Stuyvesant, bedecked and beplumed, the burgomasters, *schout* and *schepens*. At the City Hall, an old inn made

The burghers filed into the City Hall

over to house the officials of this first American city, the ceremony was concluded. So the city which is today the nation's largest is also its oldest.

However, Peter could not go all the way in this gesture to his people. He still held out against complete surrender of his authority.

It had been decreed that the burghers were to elect their officials. Peter beat them to it. He appointed them.

But he chose well. They were all Dutchmen

and all popular save one, the wily Van Tien-hoven, and that doubtful gentleman's shadowy deeds were soon to catch up with him.

The war across the ocean was still on, and all in New Netherland were banded together in the common cause of defense. At first the Dutch were victorious. They had a fine navy and two great admirals, Martin Tromp and Michael de Ruyter. They swept the English Channel clear of British ships, and to symbolize this feat tied brooms on the masts of their flagships and dared the British to come out and fight.

But later the tide began to turn, and with the turn fear grew in New Netherland.

Suddenly came news that British warships had arrived in Boston harbor carrying two hundred British regulars, who were joined by six hundred New England volunteers. There was great excitement and great consternation in New Amsterdam.

The New Englanders prepared to strike. Massachusetts demurred, but the rest of the colonists were eager to proceed against Peter and his ill-defended fort.

Then, out of the blue, came news that peace

had been declared between England and Holland. The year was 1654.

"Let us give thanks to God!" said Peter to the crowd that gathered at the fort. And they did.

Prosperity seemed just around the corner now. The burghers rallied to Peter again. Eager to build up this newest of cities, he proposed to take a trip to the West Indies to promote trade. The burgomasters and the *schepens* welcomed the idea. They were brimming with good will. They met and passed a resolution:

"Whereas," it said, "the right honorable Peter Stuyvesant, intending to depart, the burgomasters and *schepens* shall compliment him before he takes his gallant voyage, and shall for this purpose provide a gay repast on Wednesday next, in the council chamber of the City Hall."

It was gay indeed. Everyone beamed at everyone else. Peter, for his part, presented the city with an official seal having a beaver for its crest. It is still the seal of the City of New York, although the only beavers seen in the city now are in the zoo.

Peter sailed away. In a few months, though, he was back. Word had reached him of a new danger to his precious colony, this one from the south.

16

TROUBLE TO THE SOUTH

WHEN Peter sailed back into New Amsterdam harbor six months later—in July, 1655—his seas were not so calm.

There in the harbor was a Dutch warship, the *Balance,* with its thirty-four guns bristling.

Peter hurried ashore. He sent for the ship's captain.

"What's all this?" he demanded.

"We are awaiting your orders, sir," said the captain.

"Orders for what?" asked Peter.

"To proceed against the Swedes," said the captain, handing Peter a large official envelope.

Peter read the letter. His mind flashed back over the years.

Sweden long ago had planted a colony to the south of that founded by the Dutch. Originally this had been a project of Gustavus Adolphus, the great Swedish king whose armies swept Europe in the early seventeenth century. But he died on the field of battle before he could send colonists to America.

King Gustavus Adolphus was succeeded on the throne by Queen Christina. She couldn't do much planning herself, for she was only six years old. But her counselor, the wise old Count Axel Oxenstierna, saw the possibilities of a new world colony.

When, in 1637, he got around to doing something about it, he chose a Dutchman to take charge, but in the name of Sweden. It was a Dutchman we've met in these pages. It was Peter Minuit, who had been Governor of New Netherland and had been recalled.

Minuit knew this new land and knew it well. He was well aware that there was no colony between English Virginia and Dutch New Netherland. So he headed an expedition which landed and planted the Swedish flag on the shore of the Delaware River near where the city of Wilmington stands now.

The Dutch didn't like this and they protested. But Minuit was smart. It was he, you remember, who bought Manhattan Island from the Indians for twenty-four dollars in beads and buttons. Now he bought land at this new site in the same way and for more trinkets. And so the Swedes built trading posts and, eventually, a fort which they named for their Queen.

In 1643 a great hulk of a man, Lieutenant Colonel Johan Printz, arrived to govern New Sweden. He weighed more than four hundred pounds. He was a good soldier and a good diplomat. Under him the Swedes enlarged their holdings by dealing wisely with the Indians and by getting along well with the neighboring Dutch and laughing off any protests made by the New Netherland officials. But it was obvious that sooner or later there would be a clash.

This was one of the troubles, along with many others, that Stuyvesant inherited from Kieft. Peter wasn't to be smiled away so easily. His was a firmer stand. The Swedes had bought land from the Indians. He could do so too. He made a deal with Chief Peminacka for all the land on the Delaware "from Minquas Kill to the Bay." For this he paid not a bead nor a button, just a promise to mend the Chief's gun whenever it needed repair. It was quite a bargain.

Peter decided the Dutch must have a fort in this vicinity, too. So he sent soldiers and workmen to build Fort Casimir. He was stiffening his policy toward Printz. Printz knew it, too. He had only a small number of colonists. He wrote home begging for more. His government did not cooperate fully. Once they sent a shipload, but the ship was wrecked. This discouraged other colonists. It even discouraged Printz. He resigned and sailed for home.

Eventually the Swedish Government sent as his successor Johan Rising. He was ordered to take over for the Swedes the entire river, "without hostility." For by this time the Dutch weren't paying much attention to their settlement. Fort Casimir had been allowed to go to seed.

When Rising's ship, the *Orn,* arrived in the Delaware River, he was on a mission of peaceful expansion. But the party which put out to greet him told him that the time had come to attack the Dutch. They reported to him that Fort Casimir was in almost total decay.

Rising dropped anchor off the dilapidated Dutch fort and fired a salute. There was no answering salute and for good reason. There was no gunpowder in the Dutch fort.

That was all Rising wanted to know. He "let them have a couple of shots" from his heaviest guns, marched a few men into the fort, forced the weak Dutch garrison to surrender, and ran up the Swedish flag.

When Peter heard this news he was furious. But it came at a bad moment. He was preparing to defend New Amsterdam against those ships of Cromwell's in Boston harbor, which were reportedly about to attack.

So he sent off a letter to Holland asking for

instructions. Then came peace between the Dutch and the English, and Peter's trip to the Indies. Letters back and forth took weeks and even months in those days.

Now here he was, reading the answer from Holland to his request for orders. It was the answer he wanted. He was to proceed against the Swedes. Here was a warship, the *Balance,* to lead the attack.

Peter finished reading the letter.

"We shall attack at once!" he said.

Word spread through the city with the same rapidity that fire might have leaped from thatched roof to thatched roof.

Peter now was in his glory. Here was a military expedition with almost certain victory at the other end. The Swedes were outnumbered, to start with. Even the few soldiers Peter had at his command could have overwhelmed them.

But now every able-bodied man in the city wanted to join the army. It would be a sort of autumn vacation adventure. They all flocked to the colors. There was drilling with guns and even with broomsticks. Everyone who owned a ship volunteered it. Even a French ship in port joined in.

On the first Sunday in September, 1655, "after the sermon," the squadron of seven vessels with a force of about seven hundred men set forth. Peter was in command.

Five days later they were in the Delaware River. Peter sent a drummer boy ashore with an ultimatum. There was a short delay. The Dutch were ready to charge. But before they could do so the small Swedish garrison surrendered.

The Dutch moved on and surrounded Fort Christina. Rising himself commanded the fort and was prepared to fight. But his soldiers saw that the odds were against them and threatened to mutiny. There was nothing for Rising to do but surrender.

Peter had his big military victory. The Swedes were no longer to threaten him. He prepared to return to New Amsterdam in glory.

But suddenly a courier from New Amsterdam appeared on the scene bearing this message:

"Come quickly! Two thousand Indians have fallen upon us."

Poor Peter! It seemed as though his troubles never would end. He turned his ships back. His soldiers and his volunteers were no longer celebrating.

17

THE INDIANS ATTACK AGAIN

PETER found his colony trembling with fear. He rushed at once to his *bouwerie,* for he had left Judith and his two sons there unguarded.

Fortunately they were safe. Neighbors had hurried to protect them.

Then Peter turned to the big problem, for Indians in war paint were still roaming the woods with guns as well as tomahawks. Peter could not understand all this. He had gotten along well with the red men. He had treated them justly. What had happened?

It did not take long to find out.

Hendrick van Dyck, a thorn in Peter's side from the day they sailed from Holland to this new land, was the villain.

Van Dyck looked out his window one day while Peter and his army were conquering New Sweden, and he saw an Indian squaw picking his peaches. She was alone and evidently she was just hungry.

Van Dyck didn't bother to remonstrate with her. He just took his gun, opened the window, and shot her through the heart. It was a wanton killing and it was little wonder the Indians felt deeply about it.

There was no protest from them. But they knew that every able-bodied man in the colony was away with Peter, at war.

Suddenly one morning the streets of New Amsterdam were filled with two thousand painted, feathered warriors. Their war whoops filled the air. The burghers hid in their homes behind bolted doors.

Oddly enough, the Indians did little but bully and rob that first day. Perhaps this was out of respect for Peter, who had been their friend.

The next day, however, they sought out Van Dyck. A well-bowed arrow killed him. Then Paulus van der Grist, a neighbor, was felled with an ax.

There was still time for good counsel to prevail. An attempt was made to gather the Indian leaders on Governor's Island for a peace conference. But Cornelis van Tienhoven, who never had been a good influence in the colony, was no better now. Although as *schout* he should have done everything to preserve public peace, he urged the burghers to strike back.

When the Indians learned of this, they withdrew from Manhattan Island. But that night they struck on the other side of the river. They fell upon Pavonia, burning houses, killing almost every man, and taking women and children captive. One of the men who escaped carried the news to Peter in New Sweden.

The next day the Indians sacked the *bouwerie* of the dead Van Dyck, burned eleven more farmhouses, and killed many. Then they moved on to Long Island. Some spread to upper Manhattan Island. Within a few days, more than a hundred people were killed, twenty-eight *bou-*

weries desolated, and much property was destroyed, including grain for food.

Peter came back to all this devastation. Only his wisdom saved the day. If the burghers had followed Van Tienhoven's advice and attempted to fight, the city itself, which had not been touched, would have been in danger. Indians with torches could have set it ablaze.

First, Peter rallied the people from their fear. When he played the soldier he inspired confidence, for the burghers knew he was a good soldier.

To all intents and purposes he prepared for war. He ordered all ships to stay in port. He forbade any men able to fight to leave the city. He made a big show of military drills and parades.

Then, knowing the Indians were lacking in food and ammunition, and that they didn't know what to do with their many captives, he sent out peace feelers. This led to negotiations. The Indian chiefs again felt his warm personality and his great charm. In a matter of days, amid much peace-pipe smoking, a new and lasting peace treaty was signed. There was an exchange of the prisoners, whom the Indians didn't want, for the food which they did.

But Peter never completely trusted the Indians again. Perhaps what he really mistrusted was the attitude of his burghers toward them. At any rate, no red man was ever again permitted to remain overnight within the walls of New Amsterdam.

However, at least some good came out of all the bad. Cornelis van Tienhoven long had been an evil influence upon Peter. No one knows why the Governor had clung to his friendship and accepted his self-seeking and harmful aid.

Van Tienhoven's hat and cane

Now new protests against Van Tienhoven went to the West India Company's directors in Holland. This time they acted. They wrote that they believed the *schout* "with clouded brains filled with liquor" had been the "prime cause" of the recent "doleful massacre," or at least could have prevented it by "caution and good sense." They decreed that he be dismissed.

A few months later, his successor in office, Nicasius de Sille, asked permission to seize and seal his property, as he had "absconded." Not long after, his hat and cane were found floating in the river near the shore.

But such was Van Tienhoven's craftiness that no one could be sure he was dead. The burghers did see that he had no memorial, however. The name of Tienhoven Street. was changed, and he was forgotten.

18

LIFE BECOMES CALMER

THE years that immediately followed were, for the most part, happy ones. The burghers seemed to mellow. So did Peter. No longer did he stomp to the city tavern to give harsh orders to his subjects. Instead he made his way there to drink a mug of beer, and to bask in the sunshine of his new popularity.

The conflict that had torn him seemed to be easing. In 1657 he granted his subjects Great and Small Burgher Rights. Then gradually, and hardly perceptibly, as though he had been ashamed of denying them the right to elect their own officers, he granted them this freedom.

His own family fortunes were flowering, too. His *bouwerie* was a beautiful place. He loved flowers and trees, and planted many of them.

He spent as much time as possible with his family. His boys were growing up. Judith had brought them up well. Anneke, his sister, had tutored them and her own children brilliantly. Gay were the parties in the farmhouse, especially the parties for the children.

Peter found time in 1658 to build himself a house in town, too. It was the city's first great mansion. It was built of gray stone, so light in color that it was called "The White Hall." It was at the tip of Manhattan Island below the fort, at the foot of what is now Whitehall Street. Its lovely gardens, planned by Judith, were crisscrossed by prim walks bordered with box, and went right down to the water's edge. The Governor's yacht lay at what the Indians called the "safe landing place," and here distinguished visitors from abroad were welcomed.

The Governor now found the time and the inclination to institute many of the improvements of which he had dreamed for his city. From the first time he and Judith had walked through the streets of New Amsterdam, he had worried about the fire hazard.

In 1657 Peter finally imported from Holland a hundred and fifty leather buckets and commissioned the town's two shoemakers to make a hundred more like them. The buckets were distributed to strategic points.

When a fire was discovered the shout went up. Every citizen within hearing was obligated to respond. If he did not he was subject to a fine. The citizens rushed to get the buckets, filled them at the nearest spring or pump, formed lines and passed them along. The last person in line dashed water on the flames. It was our first fire department.

New Amsterdam was fortunate in those early days, for none of the plagues which sometimes swept European and Asiatic countries reached these shores. In 1658 the first hospital in the city was established. Here the ill were treated. Operations were performed by, of all people, the town barber.

Now and again the Indian menace threatened, but Stuyvesant always dealt firmly with it. On these occasions he not only displayed diplomatic ability but also physical courage.

When a farmer was killed at Esopus, and war with the red men seemed about to flare, Peter went to the scene and called for a meeting of the Indian sachems.

More than sixty of them gathered under a great oak tree. Stuyvesant went out to meet them without a guard. He asked what the trouble was. An old chief recounted the wrongs his people had suffered at the hands of the white men. Peter heard him out, then spoke:

"Has any injury been done to you since I came to this country?" he asked.

There was no answer.

Then Peter said that he wanted the Indians to surrender the murderer of the farmer. The old chief said that it was a brave of another tribe and that he had disappeared. The chief said he had nothing against the white men, but that the young Indians wanted to fight. Peter leaped to his feet.

"Let them step forth," he challenged. "I will place man against man. Yes, I will place twenty against forty of your hotheads. Now is your time. But it is unmanly and mean and contemptible to threaten farmers and women and children who are not warriors."

The Indians did not answer then. Later their answer took the form of land which they gave to found a new village on the site of the farmer's murder.

There was to be another outbreak from the red men later. But for the moment Peter probably wished the white men had been as easy to deal with, and as honorable.

To the south, the Swedes had been eliminated. But now the English from Virginia colony were "crowding out" the Dutch in a northward push, claiming jurisdiction under the very early grant to Lord Baltimore.

Connecticut and even Massachusetts (which had heretofore been somewhat friendly) now ignored completely and deliberately the boundary agreement worked out in Hartford in 1650. This was partly the fault of the Dutch in Holland, for they had delayed signing this agreement until 1656. By that time the English had become more covetous, and kept putting off ratification.

About this time a man named George Bax-

Stuyvesant went out alone to meet the Indians under a great oak tree

ter, who had once worked with Stuyvesant as English secretary of New Netherland and been forced to resign because of his treachery, tried to stir up a revolt on Long Island. He was arrested, but escaped to New England. There he was joined by Captain John Scott, who had been deported from England in an army scandal. Together they made constant trouble for the Dutch.

But even with these clouds on its horizon, New Amsterdam grew and thrived. In his new gracious role Peter expected in return the same friendship he gave. He went to Boston to try to convince the colonists that there was room for both English and Dutch in the New World. He received only evasive answers.

Peter had, from time to time, urged the homeland to give more help to building up a defense of the colony. The West India Company paid scant attention to these appeals.

After their last rebuff, he had written again to his superiors:

"Your Honors imagine that the troubles in England will prevent any attempt on these parts. Alas, they are ten to one in number to us, and able, without any resistance, to deprive us of the country when they please."

Then news came that cheered him. Cromwell had died. Power fell to his son, Richard, but not for long. Now in 1660 came word that the monarchy had been restored. Charles II had been made King.

Peter was happy. Had not the Dutch in the homeland sheltered Charles in his exile? Out of pure gratitude, thought Peter, the English King would be friendly. He was mistaken.

19

CHARLES II returned to England from his Dutch exile in 1660, and took the throne. After some austere years the English were glad to see him. They greeted him with every evidence of joy.

"I cannot see for the life of me," he remarked dryly, "why I have stayed away so long when everybody is so charmed with me now that I at length am back."

The King was young, handsome and cheerful. He was much more interested in having a good time than he was in affairs of state.

When Lord Baltimore tried to urge the King to claim for England the Dutch territory on the Delaware River, Charles wouldn't listen.

"The subject is too heavy for a crowned head," he said. "I hope I may be spared the stupid task of looking after a batch of restless Western adventurers."

But Charles was won over through his vanity, and the man responsible for changing his mind was John Winthrop, a son of the Governor of Massachusetts. Young Winthrop went to England in 1662 with a great plan. He asked for a charter for Connecticut which would give that colony the territory "bounded East by Narragansett Bay, North by the Massachusetts line, South by the sea, and West by the Pacific Ocean, including all the islands thereunto adjoining." This embraced not only New Netherland but almost everything else on this continent.

Winthrop was an elegant and brilliant courtier. At his audience with the King he wore a magnificent ring which, legend has it, had been

given to his grandmother by Charles I. He took
off the ring and, with a flourish, presented it to
the monarch. It was a sentimental gift, for
Charles loved and revered his father who had
once worn it.

At this point Winthrop asked for the charter.
Charles granted it.

When Peter heard of this he was in a fury. It
was clearly a violation of the boundary agreement of 1650. But Winthrop just laughed at him.

Peter asked his own government to protest to
Charles. He asked that Charles be reminded of
the sanctuary he had been given in Holland.

But it seems that Charles was not grateful but

Four frigates sailed from England at night

resentful. His position in Holland had been humiliating, and now he was disposed to be unfriendly. His advisors, and principally the Duke of Clarendon, realized the great future of America and wanted it all. Then there was the King's brother, the Duke of York, who had to be kept prominent and, if possible, occupied.

So in March of 1664 Charles affixed his seal to a patent by which he granted to the Duke of York "the territory comprehending Long Island and the islands in the neighborhood, and all the lands and rivers from the west side of the Connecticut River to the east side of Delaware Bay."

This included almost all of New Netherland. And it was in complete disregard of the grant the King had just made to Connecticut. Now two English factions "owned" the Dutch colony.

The Duke, who was also Lord High Admiral of the British Navy, borrowed four frigates from his brother the King, and sent them off in command of Colonel Richard Nicolls. Nicolls was also appointed vice-governor of the prospective new province, with orders to take over at once.

All of this was kept a deep secret. The vessels sailed from England under cover of darkness. Every effort was made to conceal their departure and their mission.

However, plots as big as this one are difficult to hide. There were those in Boston who knew of the coming of the frigates and boasted of a conquest near at hand. This word seeped down to New Netherland.

There was a flurry of alarm. Lookouts were posted to watch the entrance to the harbor. Peter asked his employers in Holland to find out what the dispatch of warships to America meant. Charles was wily. He explained to the Dutch minister in London that these ships were carrying bishops to New England.

The tension eased in New Amsterdam. Peter, confident now that all was well at home, set off to the north. There had been some trouble with the Indians there, and he meant to use his calming influence on the red men.

He had not been away long when couriers came to him with dismaying news.

The four English warships had arrived off New Amsterdam harbor. They were blocking the

Narrows. They had sent a detachment of soldiers ashore on Long Island to warn all inhabitants not to send supplies or assistance to the city.

Peter hurried home, heartsick.

20

SURRENDER

PETER stood on the crumbling ramparts of his shaky little fort and took stock of his situation. The fort and the walls were in a sad state of disrepair. They might have held off a few Indians but not a well-organized and civilized enemy.

He had only a few soldiers. He could not mount many guns and could not keep them booming long, because there was less than a thousand pounds of gunpowder in the city.

His spirits were indeed low. But his courage was high. The presence of the four warships constituted an outrage. He had been tricked and deceived. The English had no right to this land. It belonged to the Dutch. What was more important, Peter had learned to love it as his own.

"No," he said to Judith, who tried to calm him. "We must fight for what is right!"

His first act was to send Dominie Megapolensis to the commander of the fleet to find out what his intentions were. There might still be a possibility of reasoning for the right.

The dominie brought back a letter from Colonel Nicolls explaining his mission and demanding immediate surrender. But the Colonel had forgotten to sign the letter. And Peter was still Peter! He sent the letter back to Nicolls, refusing to recognize an unsigned demand.

Now the burghers were restless. They knew the odds against them. They met at the *Stadt Huys,* or city hall, and muttered about surrender in the hope of good terms.

A few days later Colonel Nicolls sent another

Winthrop brought a letter from Colonel Nicolls

letter, this one by John Winthrop, who rowed to shore bearing a white flag.

Peter, with his burgomasters and councilors, received him. Then Peter read the letter. It offered what the enemy called good terms: the Dutch would be given "the same privileges as His Majesty's English subjects."

Peter tore up the letter and stamped on it with his peg leg.

But now the people were more than restless. They were eager to prevent a "needless war." They had heard of the letter and demanded to see it. They stormed through the streets in mobs, shouting:

"The letter! The letter!"

Peter heard this and saw that he must do some-thing. He ordered an aide to paste the pieces of the letter together. It was then read at a public meeting. Now more than ever the populace de-manded surrender.

Colonel Nicolls, too, was becoming impatient. On September 4, 1664, he landed troops at Breuckelen, by way of warning.

Peter made not a move. The people gathered round the fort and insisted the city could not be defended.

On September 5th the flagship of Colonel Nicolls' fleet, the frigate *Guinea,* moved into the harbor off Governor's Island. All of its cannon were mounted on one side and that side was turned toward the feeble little fort. Slowly the other ships, the *Martin,* the *William and Nicho-las,* and the *Elias,* moved alongside.

As they dropped anchor, Peter stood by one of the guns of his useless fort, broken-hearted but helplessly defiant.

Word came from the fleet that he would be given forty-eight hours to surrender. He was to raise a white flag as the signal.

The people thronged about him, begging him to capitulate before the city was destroyed and many people killed. Peter didn't even turn his head.

"It is a matter of desperation rather than soldiership to hold the fort," he was told by Nicasius de Sille, Vice-Governor.

Dominie Megapolensis put his hand on Peter's shoulder.

"Do you not see," he pleaded, "that there is no help for us, either to north, south, east or west? What can our twenty guns do in the face of sixty-two pointed toward us on yonder frigate?"

Peter was silent.

The crowd pleaded again for surrender.

"I would rather be carried a corpse to my grave," said Peter.

The next day a messenger came from the *Stadt Huys* with a petition. Peter read it.

"To resist," it read, "could mean only misery, sorrow, conflagration, the dishonor of women, the murder of children in their cradles and, in a word, the destruction of about fifteen hundred innocent souls."

It was signed by the burgomasters, the *schepens,* every leading citizen—ninety-three names in all.

Peter turned to the dominie, his face streaming with tears. The dominie took his arm and led him silently away.

No one knows exactly what prompted Peter's final decision to give up his hopeless stand. Perhaps it was that on the petition, near the top of the list, was the name Balthazar Stuyvesant— Peter's own son, now seventeen.

The next day, September 7, 1664, little Fort Amsterdam surrendered.

Peter, his head erect, marched out of the fort at the head of his troops with colors flying, drums beating.

Before the sun had set, Cornelis van Ruyven, who had been secretary of the colony, had written out the announcement:

"Governor Nicolls has altered the name of the city of New Amsterdam and named the same New York."

Thus, except for a brief period later, ended the rule of the Dutch in the New World, just fifty-five years after Henry Hudson had sailed into the river which now bears his name.

And thus began the new life of a city which was to become the greatest in the world.

21

PETER'S LAST DAYS

NEW AMSTERDAM became New York easily
and gracefully so far as its inhabitants were con-
cerned. Colonel Nicolls, the new governor,
granted the colony probably the most favorable
terms ever given by a conqueror to those con-
quered.

Nor was Peter allowed to feel humiliated. His
fellow townsmen now became closer than ever to
the man who had governed them. They recog-

nized his courage, and they knew that he had shown more than just the courage to fight to the end. For it took courage to surrender, too, when his whole will was to fight an unjust attack. He was cheered when he walked through the streets.

But back in Holland it was different. The States-General resented the illegal capture of New Netherland. As a result, the Dutch fleet was sent out to harass the English. It was so successful, largely on the African coast, that Charles II declared war against the Dutch.

The Dutch West India Company was just as angry as the States-General. The company had been close to bankruptcy for several years, and the loss of the colony was a death blow to it.

But it could not die gracefully. It must have a scapegoat for this loss. It blamed Peter— Peter, who had pleaded for years for a better defense for his colony. It accused him of a "scandalous surrender," and it ordered him home for trial.

Peter sailed in the summer of 1665, with his head high. He knew he had fought a good fight. Almost every resident of New Amsterdam saw him off with cheers as well as tears.

Peter Stuyvesant was going back to Holland

He faced his accusers with his usual courage.
For a time things were extremely unpleasant.
Then letters from the lost colony began to pour
in to the States-General. They were letters of love
and affection and vindication for a grand old
man.

One was signed by the burgomasters and all
the *schepens:*

"During eighteen years of administration His
Honor has conducted and demeaned himself not
only as a director-general, according to the best
of our knowledge, ought to do on all occasions,

for the best interests of the West India Company, but besides as an honest proprietor and patriot of this province and as a supporter of the Reformed Religion."

This was from the men with whom Peter had quarreled many times and against whom he had stormed when he thought them wrong. But they were fair men and just.

The States-General heard all of this testimony. It also heard Peter's simple story. And it voted overwhelmingly to vindicate him. It even urged him to settle down in Holland and enjoy a distinguished old age.

But there were no conflicting loyalties within Peter now. He knew where his heart was—in the new land to which he had given the fine years of his stormy life.

He could not return to America at once because the war was still on between the Dutch and the English, and the seas were not safe. But the moment the Treaty of Breda was signed in 1667, he sailed. He was on the bridge, smiling, when his ship reached New York harbor.

There was an English governor in the White Hall, but Peter settled down on his *bouwerie*. His sons were grown, but he and Judith kept busy about the farm. Peter loved to plant things in this land he had chosen as his own. He puttered about his garden all day. At night he sat and read his Bible.

And then, in February of 1672, this long eventful life came to an end.

Peter was buried in a little chapel on his farm. When Judith followed him in death some years later, she left money for a church to be built on the site of the chapel. There it stands today, St. Marks-in-the-Bouwerie, in the heart of New York's lower East Side, embracing the chapel in which still lie the bones and the silver-banded leg of the last Governor of New Netherland.

New York was calm and peaceful under its new regime, but it did not take quickly to English words or English ways. Dutch continued for many years to be the predominant language. Governor Nicolls also continued the Dutch form of government, with its burgomasters, *schepens* and *schout*, for more than a year. When, in 1665, he named a mayor and sheriff and board of aldermen to replace them, four of the seven aldermen were Dutch.

However, the Government of the Netherlands

did not surrender New Amsterdam as easily as had the burghers themselves. In London the Dutch ambassador protested to Charles, and kept on protesting through the subsequent months and even years.

Governor Nicolls didn't find his task much easier than had Peter. Financial problems pressed the colony. Finally Nicolls resigned and went back to England. Even the Dutch were sorry to see him go because he had been a good governor.

The King sent Colonel Francis Lovelace to succeed him. He governed wisely, too. But by this time Charles had become a little too ambitious. He formed an alliance with Louis XIV of France, and in 1672 the two countries declared war on Holland with the hope of eliminating their most potent rival.

Again the Dutch proved themselves fine sea fighters. They pursued English men-of-war and merchantmen on all the seas.

It was on such a chase that two Dutch admirals, Cornelis Everts and Jacob Binckes, found themselves on this side of the Atlantic. Every port was now fair prey. There was a war.

And what finer prize, thought the admirals, than the port that had once been Dutch? Their fleet sailed into New York harbor in July, 1673, twenty-three ships strong. Just as the English had demanded surrender, so did they. Just as Peter had protested, so did Lovelace.

The Dutch admirals fired a broadside into the fort. They landed men just above "the governor's orchard" back of the present Trinity Church. And the English ran up a white flag.

The city was Dutch again. Its conquerors named it New Orange instead of New Amsterdam.

But there was no Peter Stuyvesant to hold it now.

A year later the Netherlands and Great Britain ended their war. In the making of the Treaty of Westminster, not even a long argument ensued over the city that should have been a prize of the first magnitude. It was ceded back to the English.

And so in November, 1674, the Dutch flag came down again and the English flag went up. There it flew for more than a hundred years, until one day a new kind of American named

George Washington, heading a rebel army, marched into the city. He claimed it in the name of a new nation under whose flag it was to rise to its greatest glory.

POSTSCRIPT

THOSE of you who live in New York today, and those who visit what is now the largest city in the Western Hemisphere, may want to relate the days of which you have been reading to those of the present. This postscript is written to help you put the two eras together.

We began by telling you that the civilized world was much smaller at the time of our story.

So was New York, or New Amsterdam, as it was known then.

The great city sprawls over all of Manhattan Island now, and stretches out beyond. But in those early days the little town occupied just the lower tip of the island.

The village of those days ended at Pearl Street on the south and east, Greenwich Street on the west, and Wall Street on the north. The land beyond those thoroughfares was reclaimed slowly and gradually in later years.

There was a Battery then, but it was not quite so far south as it is now, and it was a real battery with real guns.

Pearl Street, the southern boundary, was named because of the pearly shells picked up along the shore. The northernmost street, Wall Street, took its name from the wall, or stockade, built as a defense against the Indians and later rebuilt and made stronger by Peter Stuyvesant.

Many streets got their names for definite reasons. Whitehall Street led to Peter's fine mansion, the White Hall, and Stone Street was the first one in the little town to be paved with cobblestones. That happened in 1657. Farther north, Maiden Lane was at first a path; it followed a brook where young girls washed their clothes.

The fort, around which the town's life centered after it was built in 1626 by Peter Minuit, stood where the Customs House now stands—a full block bounded by Battery Place, Whitehall, Bridge and State streets. Within the fort was built the first church on the island.

The huts that Adriaen Block built—the first houses on the island—stood at what is now 41 Broadway.

The legend is that Peter Minuit negotiated the purchase of Manhattan Island from the Indians on the section of land now known as Bowling Green. In early Dutch days it was a market place.

The first City Hall, or *Stadt Huys,* was located at what is now 73 Pearl Street. It contained a jail, a debtor's prison and a courthouse, too.

On Stone Street, where the Produce Exchange now stands, is a plaque marking it as the site of the first school on the island.

There are many other Dutch landmarks faintly concealed by names that became Anglicized in later years:

Conyn's Island thus became Coney Island;

Sandt Hoeck, Sandy Hook; Vlachte Bos, Flatbush; Deutel Bay, Turtle Bay; Jemaico, Jamaica.

Dutch names still appear in the *City Directory* and in the telephone book. (How curiously those early settlers would have regarded the telephone!) Among them are names such as Stuyvesant, Van Renssalaer, Beekman, Verplanck, Van Cortlandt, De Peyster, Schuyler, Kip, Van Dam, Brinckerhoff, DeVries, and a very illustrious one—Roosevelt.

The Bowery, the New York street where human derelicts seem to drift, gets its name from Peter Stuyvesant's *bouwerie,* through which it ran as a path. This great farm of about six hundred acres stretched from what is now Fourth Avenue, on the west, to the river on the east, and from Sixth to Seventeenth streets.

There were other large *bouweries,* too: that of the family of Peter's sister, the Bayards, which was close by; the Kip family's along the shore of the East River in the thirties, now called Kip's Bay; and a famous one, first staked out for himself by Peter Minuit and later taken over by another governor, Wouter van Twiller, which embraced practically all of what is now Green-

Stuyvesant's name will live as long as the nation which he helped to found

wich Village. Here Van Twiller built the first house erected north of New Amsterdam.

Except for these farms, the territory north of Wall Street (the town's boundary line) was wild, almost junglelike. It was dangerous, too, for wild animals roamed about. It had lakes and streams, some of which still exist but are buried under the teeming city that has replaced the wilderness.

Heere Straat, which was to become Broadway, fought its way, after a fashion, through some of this country. Eventually the long street found its way to a village to the north which Stuyvesant founded in 1658 and called New Haarlem. It is just called plain Harlem now and is a thriving part of the metropolis. But in the early days it was a good day's journey to its center, about where 125th Street crosses First Avenue today. It must have been considered a good site for a settlement, even before the Dutch built there, for Indian arrowheads and other relics have been found in quantity in the vicinity.

Across the East River, on Long Island, there were also many early settlements, one of which, at least, has gained great prominence. It belonged to the Canarsie Indians until the white men came along and found the site attractive. They dug in and established a settlement in 1643. They called it Breuckelen. It was pronounced Brooklyn and that is the way it is spelled today.

When Peter returned from Holland to settle down to his last days in America, he brought with him a pear tree which he planted on his *bouwerie*.

"By this," he said, "my name may be remembered."

It flourished for more than two hundred years. A great city grew up around it. An iron fence was built to preserve it in the midst of New York's turbulence. At last, a few years ago, the pear tree died.

But if Peter thought his name would die with it, he was mistaken. His name will live as long as the nation which he helped to found.

Peter was a curious combination of the weaknesses and the strength of which men are made. He had his faults. He had his virtues. He could be petty and he could be great. It is curious but true, in the strange process which creates history, that with the passing of years pettiness vanishes and greatness remains. It is thus with Peter Stuyvesant.

INDEX

Andraeson, Gerrit, 50
Albany, New York, 17, 30, 33–34
Algonquin Indians, 48–49
Alphen-on-Rhine, Netherlands, 62
Amsterdam, Netherlands, 8–9, 67
Archangel, 18
Aruba (island), 56
Asia, and the route to, 6, 8, 10, 18

Balance (warship), 129, 134
Baltimore, Lord, 147, 152
Barber(s), 145
Barentsen expedition, 8
Barneveldt, Jan van Olden, 22
Battery (The), 172
Battery Place, 173
Baxter, George, 117, 119, 147–49
Bayard, Anneke Stuyvesant (sister), 62–63, 70, 144, 174
Bayard, Judith, 63–65
Bayard, Samuel, 62–63
Beads and buttons, 15, 27
Beaver(s), and beaver skins, 22, 45, 47–49, 127
Bed(s), bedrooms, 85–86, 89
Bedstee, 89
Binckes, Admiral Jacob, 168–69
Blaewe Hoen (ship), 58
Block, Captain Adriaen, 18–20, 22–24, 173
Bogardus, Everardus, 31, 43, 51–52, 98
Boston, Massachusetts, 126, 133, 149, 155
Bouweries, 41, 50, 137, 139–40, 144, 174–76

Bowery (street), 174
Bowling Green (street), 91, 173
Bradford, Governor William, 29, 112–13
Brazil, 38, 56–57
Breda, Netherlands, 66
Breda, Treaty of, 166
Breuckelen. See Brooklyn
Bridge Street, 173
Broadway, 176
Brooklyn, New York, 91, 160, 177
Buen Aire (island), 56
Burghers, 29–30, 73, 76–77, 80–81, 83–84, 86, 90, 92, 103–07, 111, 119, 121–22, 125, 127, 138–41, 143, 158, 168
Burgomaster(s), 122, 124, 127, 161, 165

Cabot, Henry, 7
Canarsie Indians, 177
Caribbean Sea, 71
Carpet(s), 88–89
Carpsey, Gabriel, 83
Cellar(s), 87
Charles I, King of England, 122, 153
Charles II, King of England, 150–53, 155, 168
Christiaansen, Captain Hendrick, 18–20, 23
Christina, Queen of Sweden, 130
Church(es), 31, 43, 51, 76, 78, 90–91, 173
City Hall, 124, 127, 158, 161, 173
Civilized world, 3, 171
Clarendon, Duke of, 153

179